AN AFRICAN DREAM

An African Dream

The History of an Evangelical Seminary for French-Speaking Africa

∽

JOHN F. ROBINSON

WIPF & STOCK · Eugene, Oregon

AN AFRICAN DREAM
The History of an Evangelical Seminary for French-Speaking Africa

Copyright © 2025 John F. Robinson. All rights reserved. Except for brief quotations in critical publications or reviews, no part of this book may be reproduced in any manner without prior written permission from the publisher. Write: Permissions, Wipf and Stock Publishers, 199 W. 8th Ave., Suite 3, Eugene, OR 97401.

Wipf & Stock
An Imprint of Wipf and Stock Publishers
199 W. 8th Ave., Suite 3
Eugene, OR 97401

www.wipfandstock.com

PAPERBACK ISBN: 979-8-3852-4192-7
HARDCOVER ISBN: 979-8-3852-4193-4
EBOOK ISBN: 979-8-3852-4194-1

"FATEB's first fifty years comprise a history of indigenous initiative, global cooperation, institutional adaptability, and divine provision. For evangelical educators and missiologists with ears to hear, Robinson's chronicle is an inspiring and instructive case study, full of ordinary yet faithful humanity."
—Daniel J. Treier, Knoedler Professor of Theology, Wheaton College

"This book provides the kind of detailed, informed, organized, and chronologically clear history that is lacking for too many evangelical institutions in the non-Western world. Its account is especially good for the key African leaders who got the Bangui Evangelical School of Theology (Central African Republic) off the ground and have made it a thriving success to this day. It is equally informative concerning the Western missionaries, including the book's author, who assisted the Africans in their sometimes complicated, often discouraging, but always faithful efforts. The book is a landmark for charting the course of evangelical theological education in an emerging center of rapid Christian development."
—Mark Noll, author of *Clouds of Witnesses: Christian Voices from Africa and Asia*

"In *An African Dream*, veteran theologian and missionary to Africa, John Robinson, tells the compelling story of the founding and impact of the first evangelical seminary in Francophone Africa: la Faculté de Théologie Évangélique de Bangui (FATEB). Robinson skillfully weaves together the themes of human agency and God's providence in bringing to life a vision once held by the esteemed Byang Kato. The story of FATEB involves triumphs, trials, breakthroughs, betrayals, resilience, and resistance—elements that define a missionary enterprise. If you are interested in church history in French-speaking Africa, the organizational lifecycle of Christian ministries, and effective partnerships between the Global North and Global South, this book is a valuable read. I highly recommend it."
—Kailu Makaya Kumbu, International Strategy Director, Development Associates International

"Meticulously researched and beautifully written, *An African Dream* presents us with an inspirational case study of courageous vision, human perseverance, and divine intervention. Dr. Robinson has given us a compelling resource for any reader endeavoring to understand what true kingdom-building partnership in global mission looks like."
—Paul Borthwick, author of *Western Christians in Global Mission: What's the Role of the North American Church?*

"In 1973, leaders of the Association of Evangelicals in Africa, itself only a few years old, saw the need for advanced theological studies—in Africa, for Africans, and by Africans. It was a bold vision, especially for evangelicals in Francophone Africa, where leaders with advanced education were perhaps only a half-dozen in number. Fulfilling that vision took courage and persistence, without much promise of organizational and financial resources. Histories of colleges and seminaries are usually rather placid, if not dull. Not this one. *An African Dream* recounts the rise and development of the Bangui Evangelical School of Theology (BEST) during army mutinies, presidential coups, the HIV-AIDS pandemic, and the struggles of everyday life in the Central African Republic—not to mention churchly intrigue and attempted theological coups. Through these many dangers, toils, and snares, BEST has come to be an exemplary theological school, and Jack Robinson shows how it got there, carefully detailing this story, step by step. This pioneering work makes an important contribution to the history of Christian development in modern Africa."

—JOEL CARPENTER, Senior Research Fellow, Nagel Institute,
Calvin University

"It is rare that the history of a theological institution can be told by someone who has been intimately involved for fifty years. Jack Robinson allows us close-up view in the development of one of the leading theological institutions for French-speaking Africa, a vibrant part of Christianity worldwide that often remains outside the purview of anglophone Christianity. This history of FATEB is at the same time the story of how African Christianity developed during and after the waning of the protestant missionary era. It also shows how African evangelicalism grew in the expression of its own theological voice so that it could properly address contextual challenges that Western theologians working in the region too often neglected or misunderstood."

—BENNO VAN DEN TOREN, Former Professor of Systematic Theology,
FATEB

Dedicated to the graduates of FATEB and their families,
and to all those whom they serve in Francophone Africa.

Contents

Abbreviations | xi
Preface: Reasons for a history of the Bangui Evangelical School of Theology/
    Faculté de Théologie Évangélique de Bangui (FATEB) | xiii
Acknowledgments | xvii

Chapter 1: African Independence and the Evangelicals—1960 to 1973 | 1

Chapter 2: Vision of a Training Institution—Byang Kato | 4
    1973–1974: Finding a Location for FATEB | 4
    1974–1975: Constructing the First Building | 14
    1975–1976: Designing the Seminary Curriculum | 18

Chapter 3: First Years of Classes—Paul White | 24
    1976–1977: Appointing FATEB's First Doyen | 24
    1977–1978: Beginning of Seminary Classes | 25
    1978–1979: Confronting Leadership Conflict | 31
    1979–1980: Expansion of FATEB's Campus | 37
    1980–1981: Adding Professors and Buildings | 41

Chapter 4: Early African Leaders—Josaphat Paluku, Isaac Zokoué | 42
    1981–1982: Graduating the First Students | 42
    1982–1983: Leadership Transitions | 44
    1983–1984: Generous Help from FATEB Friends | 46
    1984–1985: Completion of a Three-Story Academic Building | 49
    1985–1986: Struggling over Diverse Theological Views | 52
    1986–1987: Appointment of a New Doyen | 54
    1987–1988: Renewed Vision for FATEB | 60
    1988–1989: Coping with HIV/AIDS | 62
    1989–1990: Updating a Five-Year Plan | 68

Contents

1990–1991: Faculty Changes and Economic Assistance | 69
1991–1992: Signs of FATEB's Growing Impact in Francophone Africa | 70
1992–1993: Betrayal Within the Campus Community | 73
1993–1994: Critical Need for Student Scholarship Funds | 74
1994–1995: Practical Value of Visiting Professors | 77
1995–1996: Military Insurrection and Evacuation of FATEB Personnel | 80
1996–1997: Students Graduate Despite Outbreaks of Violence | 83
1997–1998: FATEB Undertakes New Projects During a Year of Peace | 86
1998–1999: Conflicts in Bordering Countries Impact Students at FATEB | 89
1999–2000: Three-Story Construction Supervised by Missionary Ken Landrud | 90

Chapter 5: Broadening the Vision—Abel Ndjéraréou, Nupanga Weanzana | 93

2000–2001: Training in Bible Translation Added to FATEB's Curriculum | 93
2001–2002: Trauma Workshops Organized | 98
2002–2003: Government Coup d'Etat, FATEB Security Compromised | 100
2003–2004: Financial Crisis, but Rescue by Generous Friends | 101
2004–2005: Doctoral Program Launched; New Buildings for the Primary School | 103
2005–2006: Team from Wheaton Bible Church Does Campus Renovations | 104
2006–2007: Ministry to Muslims Training | 105
2007–2008: Nupanga Weanzana Appointed Doyen | 106
2008–2009: HIV/AIDS Conference Conducted at FATEB | 109
2009–2010: Distance Education Program in Christian Leadership | 112
2010–2011: Annual Visits to Graduates in Ministry Begin a Second Decade | 113
2011–2012: Constructing a Conference Center for Continuing Education | 114
2012–2013: Coup d'État Sends Many FATEB Students to Cameroon Campus | 116
2013–2014: Internally Displaced People Flee to FATEB's Campus in Bangui | 119
2014–2015: After 41 Years of Service to FATEB, Isaac Zokoué Dies | 122
2015–2016: FATEB's Schools for Youth Keep Growing | 124
2016–2017: C.A.R. President Touadéra Speaks at FATEB's Fortieth Anniversary | 126

2017–2018: The Women's School Opens to Women from Bangui Churches | 127
2018–2019: Key People Join FATEB's Administrative Staff | 129
2019–2020: New Leadership Conference Center | 132

Chapter 6: Planning for the Future | 136
2020–2021: Online Master's Program Launched | 136
2021–2022: Student Enrollment Continues to Grow | 138
2022–2024: FATEB's 50-Year Anniversary of Its Charter | 139

Afterword | 143
Appendix: Western Christian Missionaries and African Christian Nationals at FATEB | 145
Appendix of Primary Sources | 147
Bibliography | 151

Abbreviations

ABI	Africa's BEST, Inc. (an American organization supporting FATEB)
ACTEA	Association for Christian Theological Education in Africa
AEA	Association of Evangelicals in Africa (current name of AEAM)
AEAM	Association of Evangelicals of Africa and Madagascar
AEC	*Alliance des Églises Évangéliques en Centrafrique* (same association as AEEC)
AEEC	*Association des Églises Évangéliques en Centrafrique*
AEO	Africa Evangelical Office
BEST	Bangui Evangelical School of Theology (English acronym for FATEB)
C.A.R.	Central African Republic
CBFMS	Conservative Baptist Foreign Mission Society
DAI	Development Associates International
D.R. Congo	The Democratic Republic of the Congo
ECFA	Evangelical Committee for Africa
EFMA	Evangelical Foreign Missions Association
FATEB	*Faculté de Théologie Évangélique de Bangui*
GBU	Groupes Bibliques Universitaires
IFMA	Interdenominational Foreign Missions Association
TEE	Theological Education by Extension
WEA	World Evangelical Alliance
WEF	World Evangelical Fellowship (later known as WEA)

Preface

Reasons for a history of the Bangui Evangelical School of Theology/Faculté de Théologie Évangélique de Bangui (FATEB)

ONLY A FEW PEOPLE remain who were present in January 1973, at the Second General Assembly of the Association of Evangelicals of Africa and Madagascar (AEAM) in Limuru, Kenya. During that meeting, a decision was made to found two university-level theological schools in Africa, one for the French-speaking countries and the other for English-speaking countries. I attended that General Assembly, and since then I have been closely associated with the francophone seminary conceived at that time. Correspondence and other documents in my files from those years have given me the sources needed for writing the following account of its history.

To my knowledge, no one has previously made a serious attempt to write a history of the francophone seminary, known in Africa under the French acronym of FATEB. With each passing year, older sources for producing such a history become more difficult to find. I have used the materials at my disposal to explain how the school was founded and then to describe some of the people and events that marked its development over the ensuing years.

In addition to writing about FATEB's history, I have retained most of the sources that I used. I hope to make them available to other researchers, once a permanent place for locating this archival material can be found.

Among those who might benefit from reading this historical account would be those in the governance structure of FATEB, as well as current and future administrators and faculty members of the seminary. This history could assist in communicating the school's identity to new personnel who join the FATEB community. It may also interest many of the institution's alumni, friends, and financial contributors.

Any institution needs to innovate to stay in step with the changes that occur within it and in the context that surrounds it. Some changes will strengthen the ability of an institution to fulfill its mission. Other changes may alter its direction so that it pursues goals that were not conceived of or intended by its founders. The leaders of FATEB, both present and future, should be able to see more clearly how FATEB's future development is linked with the values and purposes of those who founded this school. Such understanding could assist FATEB to facilitate the use of its resources and reputation in its service to Christian churches and African societies.

Plans for founding FATEB were made under the direction of Dr. Byang Kato, general secretary of AEAM. He established AEAM's Theological Commission that was responsible to oversee the process of making these plans become a reality.

In 1977, in Bangui, capital city of the Central African Republic, a former French colony, the first of the two projected educational institutions opened its doors to students. It had taken four and a half years to complete the preparations for enrolling the first class of students. Early leaders needed to obtain property, construct an academic building, find professors, and build student housing before school began. As a member of the Theological Commission, I was able to track key events of FATEB's development until the first graduation ceremony in 1982 and to write an historical narrative for that period.[1]

To record FATEB's history beyond 1982, I searched in vain for someone to who might continue to describe the school's educational work in francophone Africa. FATEB's Doyen (President) Dr. Nupanga Weanzana encouraged me to keep working on the historical narrative. I possessed several file boxes of documentary sources, but they were not comprehensive. The paper trails became even more scarce with the use of electronic files, beginning in the mid-1990s. Consequently, the resulting narrative leaves unfilled information gaps. Perhaps others may be able to answer some of the additional historical questions not addressed here.

In the following narrative are references to two different countries with Congo in their names. The Republic of Congo is a former French colony whose capital city is Brazzaville, located on the north side of the

---

1. This narrative was published in InSights Journal for Global Theological Education, Summer Supplement, August 2021.

Preface

Congo River. The second Congo lies on the south side of the Congo River. Its major city is Kinshasa, capital of the Democratic Republic of Congo, a former Belgian colony, often called the D.R. Congo. Between 1971 and 1997, its name was changed to Zaire. The following narrative refers to it as Zaire when the events of that period are described, but Zaire and the D.R. Congo denote the same country.

I began teaching at FATEB as a visiting professor in 1983 and was joined by my wife, Theo, in 1988. We continued our teaching visits to Bangui until 1994 when we moved residentially to the campus to serve as full-time professors through 1999, serving at the same time as members of an American mission agency, WorldVenture. We then resumed our annual visits to teach at the seminary, finally ending in 2012.

Acknowledgments

FATEB GREW OUT OF an African association of Evangelical Christians meeting in Kenya in 1973. Although missionary representatives of countries outside of Africa attended that gathering, the vision for creating both a French-speaking and an English-speaking graduate school of theology was clearly an African dream. The story of this book describes the founding and growth of one of these two schools, the one that now serves the Christian churches in francophone Africa. It highlights the indispensable contributions of the Africans who labored in the beginning to create FATEB, and with their colleagues, as well as their successors, to manage it successfully over five decades.

What this historical narrative does not fully reveal is the crucial partnership this institution has enjoyed with individuals, churches, and foundations outside of Africa. Some of them are mentioned briefly in the text of this history, or in a footnote, but most of them remain unnamed. Their financial support, their personal encouragement of the school's leaders, their willingness to endorse this seminary and to recommend its support to other people have been critical to the achievement of the vision of FATEB's African founders. Some have traveled to Bangui as visiting professors to assist students directly through their teaching. Others have come to make physical upgrades to one or the other of its two campuses.

While it is impossible to name all those who have helped to sustain this project over the past 50 years, it is possible to name the countries from which they and their support have come. Christians in Germany, the Netherlands, Great Britain, Sweden, Belgium, France, Switzerland, Australia, Canada, and the United States have all shared in this African project of Christian leadership development. They have offered their prayers, their gifts, their encouragement, and their love to FATEB's leaders and students, even at times when the very existence of FATEB was being challenged by outside political and military forces. These faithful friends have been indispensable to the training of hundreds of African men and women now serving in Christian leadership roles throughout Central and West Africa.

Few of these friends of FATEB realize how great an impact they have made to the strengthening of the church of Jesus Christ in francophone Africa. In our visits to FATEB alumni in various African countries my wife, Theo, and I have seen the fruit of their generosity and of their trust in the African leaders of the seminary. We wish to acknowledge the enduring significance of the essential contributions made by these caring friends. To each of them, we want to convey our heartfelt thanks.

CHAPTER 1

African Independence and the Evangelicals—1960 to 1973

FATEB OPENED ITS DOORS to French-speaking students in October of 1977. Located in Bangui, the capital city of the Central African Republic, it has now completed 48 years of training French-speaking African men and women for service in the churches and societies of Central Africa, West Africa, and Madagascar.[1] To understand why FATEB was founded and how it was launched requires a knowledge of the people, institutions, and religious movements that formed its background well before FATEB welcomed its first students.

The death of Scottish missionary and explorer David Livingstone in 1873 marked a historical moment prior to the beginning of a movement known as the Scramble for Africa, 1885–1914. Representatives of several European countries and the United States met in Berlin in 1884–1885 to decide how to conduct the colonization of Africa. During that period, Belgium, France, Germany, Italy, Portugal, Spain, and the United Kingdom took territory and power from African states and peoples. By 1914, only Liberia and Ethiopia remained independent of the colonizing nations.

Between 1957 and 1962, most African states finally regained their sovereignty. In 1960 alone, 17 countries in sub-Saharan Africa gained independence from European colonial powers. Benin, Niger, Burkina Faso, and the Côte d'Ivoire became independent in a single week, August 1–7, 1960.

---

1. AEAM, Minutes of the business sessions of the 1977 Third General Assembly, Bouaké, Côte d'Ivoire [Ivory Coast], appendix F, 2: "The GST (Graduate School of Theology) for French Africa, the Bangui Evangelical School of Theology (BEST) is to officially open October 15, 1977."

An African Dream

With political independence from the colonial powers, African churches began to grow more rapidly. African Christians began to exert greater leadership in their churches, and they began to strengthen their relationships with one another across Africa.

In 1966, a continent-wide conference of African Christian leaders was sponsored through the joint effort of two North American mission associations: the Evangelical Foreign Missions Association (EFMA), whose members were composed of denominational mission agencies, and the Interdenominational Foreign Missions Association (IFMA), whose members were mission agencies without denominational affiliations.[2] These two mission associations worked together in Africa through a bureau called the Africa Evangelical Office (AEO) that organized the African conference of 1966. At this meeting, African Christian leaders decided to create an association of African Christians called the Association of Evangelicals of Africa and Madagascar (AEAM). After nearly 60 years, its membership today is composed of national Evangelical fellowships in most African nations. Headquartered in Nairobi, Kenya, it is currently known as the Association of Evangelicals in Africa (AEA).[3]

What motivated the leaders of the EFMA and the IFMA mission associations to organize the conference in 1966 was the fear that the fast-growing ecumenical movement in Africa would introduce theological liberalism into the theologically conservative Evangelical African churches. They saw

---

2. AEAM, today called AEA, is a regional member of the World Evangelical Alliance (WEA). The World Evangelical Alliance, first called World Evangelical Fellowship, was founded at the International Convention of Evangelicals held in the Netherlands, August 5–11, 1951, with the national Evangelical Alliance of Great Britain as the founding member with the longest history of its own. This British Evangelical Alliance had been formed in Manchester, England, in November of 1846, the same year as several other national Evangelical alliances. So, FATEB was founded by AEAM (AEA) whose organizational links go back 179 years to 1846. See Howard, *Dream That Would Not Die*, 14 and 29; also Calver, *Evangelicals*, 133. For background on the IFMA, EFMA, and AEO (Africa Evangelical Office), see Breman, *Association of Evangelicals in Africa*, 7–14 (hereafter cited as *AEA*). See also Frizen, *75 Years of IFMA, 1917–1992*, on the formation of IFMA Africa Committee, 216–18; Formation of joint EFMA-IFMA Evangelical Committee for Africa (ECFA); and creation of the Africa Evangelical Office (AEO), 286–94.

3. On the fifth day of the Africa Evangelical Conference held in Limuru, Kenya, January 29 to February 6, 1966, "Dr. Aaron B. Gamedze, Vice-President of the Bantu Evangelical Church of Swaziland, proposed the creation of an African Evangelical Association. After a short debate the delegates unanimously approved this motion. The Conference ended in establishing the Association of Evangelicals of Africa and Madagascar (AEAM)." See Breman, *AEA*, 14–17.

a need for developing an African Evangelical association of churches that would promote spiritual unity based on sound biblical doctrine. They hoped such an association would assist the churches to stay faithful to biblical teaching. To this end, the Africa Evangelical Office (AEO) of the two North American mission associations sponsored several conferences throughout Africa. The AEO adopted a confession of faith borrowed from that of the Evangelical Alliance in Great Britain, founded 120 years earlier in 1846. Out of the AEO conference held in Limuru, Kenya, in 1966, the Association of Evangelicals of Africa and Madagascar, AEAM, was born.

In 1973, AEAM held its second General Assembly in Limuru, Kenya. It was at this gathering that the idea of creating Evangelical graduate level seminaries in Africa was discussed.[4] FATEB was only a vision in 1973. The idea of such an institution dedicated to the training of African leaders reflected a stream of Protestant life and thought growing out of a long Evangelical Christian tradition in nineteenth-century Great Britain, other European countries, and several countries in sub-Saharan Africa.

4. Breman, *AEA*, 12–14.

CHAPTER 2

Vision of a Training Institution—Byang Kato

1973-1974: FINDING A LOCATION FOR FATEB

THE INDIVIDUAL MOST DIRECTLY responsible for the founding of FATEB was a 37-year-old Nigerian, Byang Kato, who, in 1973, was finishing his ThD at Dallas Theological Seminary in Texas.[1] Kato had been born in northern Nigeria in 1936. After his birth, Kato's father dedicated him to be a juju priest (a man versed in traditional spiritual medicines) in the African religion of his tribe. As Kato grew older, his father instructed him in fetish practices. At age 12, against his father's wishes, Kato began attending a Sudan Interior Mission primary school. There, his teacher told the biblical story of Noah and the ark. Listening intently to his teacher, Kato felt that he needed to enter the boat of salvation, just as Noah had done. Consequently, he made a public commitment to follow Jesus Christ. Five years later, Kato dedicated his life to God for whatever he believed God wanted him to do. Two years after that, he went to Igbaja Bible College in Nigeria to prepare for Christian ministry.

At age 21, Kato married Jummai Rahila and later became the father of a girl and two boys. In 1963 he enrolled in London Bible College. After graduation, he taught at Igbaja Theological Seminary and then was elected general secretary of the Evangelical Church of West Africa (ECWA), a denomination of 1,400 Nigerian churches composed of about 400,000 people at that time. Realizing his need for more advanced education, in 1970 Kato became the first African student to enroll in Dallas Theological Seminary in

---

1. The biographical information on Kato that follows in the next three paragraphs reflects Christina Breman's research. See Breman, *AEA*, 40–47. See also Maillefer, *Memoirs*.

the USA. By 1973 Kato had completed his doctoral classes and was headed back to Nigeria.[2]

On his way, home Kato stopped in Kenya to present a paper at the AEAM Christian Education Strategy Conference in Limuru. He stayed another week to attend the Second General Assembly of AEAM, the organization that had been founded seven years earlier in 1966. At the AEAM meeting, Kato was chosen to be the first African general secretary of the association, replacing the American general secretary, Kenneth Downing. He was also appointed executive secretary of the AEAM's Theological Commission that was formed during that meeting. Because Kato was greatly needed to teach at Igbaja Theological Seminary in Nigeria, he served as a visiting professor there for several months each year over the next two years. In addition, Kato traveled widely throughout Africa on behalf of AEAM, speaking wherever he went and encouraging the formation of national Evangelical associations. He was a presenter at the International Congress on World Evangelization held in Lausanne, Switzerland, in 1974. Kato accepted a post on the executive committee of the World Evangelical Fellowship (WEF) and chaired its Theological Commission. For a young man in his thirties, these many appointments involved considerable responsibility. But as a Hausa proverb puts it, "If the camel is large, its load is great."

Out of the 1973 General Assembly of AEAM came a decision to establish two graduate schools of theology in Africa. Kato was the originator of this proposal, but he also obtained the backing of AEAM for it. A careful reading of the minutes of the General Assembly reveals no formal action with respect to these schools. However, the General Assembly's approval of a Theological Commission,[3] with Byang Kato as its executive secretary,[4] gave him the freedom he needed to proceed with this project. Appendix C of the General Assembly minutes spells out the objectives of the

---

2. Kato was awarded the ThD degree in absentia in 1974, and his dissertation was published in 1975 as *Theological Pitfalls in Africa*. See Breman, *AEA*, 46.

3. De l'Assemblée Générale Procès-Verbal des Séances Administratives de 1973, 4.

See also AEAM, Minutes of the Second General Assembly, 1973, Theological Commission: Draft terms of reference, a 1973 document from the AEAM office listing the seven secretaries appointed to the Theological Commission: Rev. Byang H. Kato, executive secretary; Rev. Fred Holland, theological education (anglophone); Dr. Paul White, theological education (francophone), Rev. Marshall Southard, academic accreditation; Rev. René Daidanso, theological research (francophone); Mr. John T. Dean, higher theological education (English); Dr. Jack Robinson, higher theological education (French).

4. Breman, *AEA*, 47.

Theological Commission. Among the seven objectives listed, point D reads as follows: "Promote advanced studies up to the level of master's and doctoral degrees."[5] So, through the action of the Theological Commission that he chaired, Kato began preparing for the founding of the two seminaries.

Kato knew there was wide and strong support for this project. In a report on the AEAM General Assembly written by its administrative secretary, Eric Maillefer, two paragraphs were devoted to the proposed schools. The report revealed the interest shown by the assembly participants in this project as the following extract indicates:

> The need for university level theological education was discussed several times during the Assembly. A Theological Commission under the direction of Pastor Byang Kato has launched an ambitious project that will lead to the foundation of two university level schools of theological education: one for francophone Africa and the other for anglophone Africa. These schools will require the baccalaureate as the condition for admission. [This was the French diploma representing successful completion of the state examination at the end of secondary school.] It is presumed that this project will be completed by September 1975.
>
> The necessity for having such schools on African soil was underlined by Mr. Kato who mentioned the danger of syncretism and universalism that becomes more and more evident among our people because of the mediocre teaching by our leaders. Having recently visited several departments of theology in African universities, Mr. Kato declared that in most of them, the teaching of these schools is far from reflecting a biblical position. "Many of these schools seem to be searching for a peaceful coexistence between the different religions of Africa," declared Mr. Kato. "After having discussed with a number of students and professors in these universities, I discovered that the general feeling was that all the world will eventually be saved, regardless of what they believe."[6]

Before the assembly ended, Kato had appointed seven secretaries within the Theological Commission that included two secretaries responsible for action on the proposed schools. In a document entitled "Africa School for Higher Education," Kato announced the appointment of Mr. John Dean

---

5. Procès-Verbal des Séances [Minutes] 1973, appendice C, 1: Commission Théologique de l'A.E.A.M., III. Objectifs: D. Promouvoir les études avancées allant jusqu'au niveau des licences et doctorats.

6. Eric Maillefer, Mini-rapport sur l'Assemblée Générale AEAM, 2. (Author's translation of the French text.)

Vision of a Training Institution — Byang Kato

as anglophone secretary and of me as francophone secretary. A job description followed, beginning with these first two points of responsibility for each of these two secretaries: (a) liaison between the proposed schools and AEAM; (b) feasibility study on location, site, students, and staff.[7]

A budget for each of the schools was also made:

Capital Expenses:	Buildings	$300,000
	Library	$75,000
Recurrent Expenses for Five Years:		$125,000
	Total for each school:	$500,000[8]

Byang Kato's leadership was essential to the action taken by AEAM's Theological Commission to establish these schools. His work in promoting them was filled with enthusiasm and energy. This quote from Kato summarizes the case he sought to make for these institutions:

> To me, the great need in Africa today is ministerial training, coupled with in-depth teaching in the church. We should make an effort to convince missionaries and Christian leaders that while evangelism should not be neglected, teaching the converts we already have should be our priority. A well-taught Christian will become an evangelist.[9]

By the time the Third General Assembly of AEAM was held in Bouaké, Côte d'Ivoire, July 30 to August 2, 1977, the francophone school was ready to open in the Central African Republic, and work on the anglophone school in Kenya was well under way. That these schools had been deeply embraced by the constituency of AEAM was apparent in the opening address at Bouaké by AEAM's president, Samuel Odunaike:

> Our Graduate Schools of Theology are meant to put the foregoing [plans] into contemporary thought and language, clothed with the correct academic syllabuses. Furthermore, Africa does not wish to be drawn into the unhealthful divisiveness of our brethren in Europe and America even though some of them are well-meaning.

---

7. AEAM, Minutes of the Second General Assembly, 1973, Theological Commission: Draft terms of reference, with attached unpublished documents cited here from the 1977 General Assembly; I received this from Maillefer.

8. AEAM, Minutes of the Second General Assembly, 1973, Theological Commission: Draft terms of reference.

9. Breman, *AEA*, 253.

> One thing which this Assembly must not overlook is the need to ensure that the strongest possible link exists between our Graduate Schools of Theology and AEAM. We should not establish the schools and abandon them to scholars whose sole preoccupation is academic excellence. The schools must be seen to operate under the overall umbrella of AEAM without losing their academic independence.[10]

Expectations for AEAM and its projects were expressed in the words of Kato and Odunaike above. They touch on at least half a dozen contextual issues that the creation of these graduate schools could help to address. Administrative Secretary Eric Maillefer noted Kato's reference to the danger of syncretism and universalism. Kato wrote extensively on these two issues in his doctoral dissertation, published in 1975 as *Theological Pitfalls in Africa*.

"Universalism means the belief that all men will eventually be saved whether they believe in Christ now or not," Kato wrote.[11] "Syncretism means combining the elements of many religions into one."[12] In the first chapter of his book, Kato describes ten factors that encourage and foster these trends. He concluded his book with a ten-point proposal for "safeguarding biblical Christianity in Africa."[13] Point three of his proposal highlighted the need for serious theological education:

> Concentrate effort in the training of men in the Scriptures, employing the original languages to facilitate their ability in exegeting the Word of God. In-depth knowledge rather than mere superficial mechanics in the ministry should be the primary concern.[14]

Defending the integrity of an Evangelical vision of Christianity against universalism, syncretism, and other theological threats was a significant priority for Kato in the African context. For him, that challenge underlined the urgent need for high quality theological education.[15]

The "mediocre teaching by our leaders" was another argument of Kato's for higher quality ministerial education. With the proliferation and

---

10. Breman, *AEA*, 253n5, from AEAM, President Samuel Odunaike quote, *Afroscope* 13 (Oct. 1977) 4.

11. Kato, *Pitfalls*, 11.

12. Kato, *Pitfalls*, 134.

13. Kato, *Pitfalls*, 181–84.

14. Kato, *Pitfalls*, 182–83.

15. For a discussion of the meaning of "Evangelical," see Howard, *Dream*, chapter 1, "Who Is an Evangelical?," 1–5.

growth of Christian churches all over Africa, many African Christian communities lacked well trained leadership. With most African nations gaining their political independence around 1960, the role of foreign missionaries from outside Africa was being replaced by African Christians who had not had the opportunities for the level of theological education enjoyed by most foreign missionaries. Kato and the AEAM believed that graduate schools of theology in Africa would produce men and women who in turn could contribute to improving the education of local church leaders.

Another issue for Kato was the eternal state of people without a belief in Christ. Kato wrote that until the mid-twentieth century, "home churches and mission boards sending missionaries overseas held a firm belief in Jesus Christ as the only way of salvation."[16] He then quoted Harold Lindsell's article stating that "the forward movement in foreign missions was based upon an implicit conviction that those outside of Christ were perishing and that if they did not hear the gospel they were lost forever."[17] In his comment above, Kato argued that "a well-taught Christian will become an evangelist." Hence, good ministerial training and in-depth teaching in the church were essential to the conduct of its evangelistic outreach.

President Odunaike, in his remarks about the creation of graduate schools of theology, pointed out the problem of ecclesiastical divisions in Europe and North America. His hope was that the new schools would not perpetuate such divisions in Africa. He emphasized the need for Evangelical unity. As will be seen, during the first year of the school's operation in Bangui, such divisions did occur and severely threatened the viability and effectiveness of the francophone graduate school project.

Odunaike also warned against an exclusive preoccupation with academic excellence. His emphasis on the need of the schools to be closely linked to AEAM reflects the fact that AEAM was an organization composed of national associations of churches. AEAM existed to serve those churches. Odunaike was committed to seeing AEAM's theological institutions committed to that same objective, namely, serving the churches in Africa.

Underlying these various motivations on the part of those who founded FATEB was the fact that the kind of institution they were envisioning did not yet exist in francophone Africa. When Christina Breman was writing

---

16. Kato, *Pitfalls*, 11.

17. Kato, *Pitfalls*, 11, citing Harold Lindsell, "Universalism Today," *Bibliotheca Sacra*, 121 (July 1964) 210.

her doctoral dissertation on the Association of Evangelicals in Africa in the early 1990s, she wrote the following comments about the school that AEAM had founded in Bangui:

> BEST [the English acronym for FATEB] is the only academic school of theology which is clearly Evangelical and committed to serving the *whole* of francophone Evangelical Africa. Other similar Evangelical schools have a more regional function. . . . BEST [FATEB] offers "training of trainers." It trains students to function as leaders of a Bible school or a regional seminary or college, which offer regular pastors' training. This is an important and necessary function, the more so since Christianity is growing in Africa.[18]

The need for such an institution as FATEB was especially great in Africa's French-speaking countries. For this reason, FATEB was selected to be the first of the two AEAM schools to be founded. "Priority was given to French-speaking Africa because anglophone Africa had about ten times as many Evangelical theological institutions, seminaries, and Bible schools as francophone Africa."[19]

The General Assembly of AEAM, held in Limuru, Kenya, February 1–8, 1973, brought together 162 delegates from 27 African countries plus observers from India, USA, Great Britain, and Germany. By this time, nine national Evangelical fellowships in Africa had been formed, of which eight were represented at the Limuru Assembly.[20] There was a strong emphasis on Christian education throughout the meetings. The assembly formed a Christian Education Commission, naming Roger E. Coon as its coordinator. The Theological Commission created by this assembly strongly supported programs of Theological Education by Extension (TEE) that had been functioning for several years under the leadership of Fred Holland in anglophone Africa and Dr. Paul White in francophone Africa. "TEE, through its study books, would enable a pastor to stay at home, continue his ministry while furthering his theological education."[21] But Kato was con-

---

18. Breman, *AEA*, 254.

19. Breman, *AEA*, 253, citing *ACTEA Directory of Theological Schools in Africa*, published in 1985, and *ACTEA Directory Supplement*, 1988.

20. For details on this assembly, see Breman, *AEA*, 68–70. See also the unpublished Maillefer, *Memoirs*, 218–19; and Eric Maillefer, mini-report on the 1973 AEAM General Assembly, 1.

21. Maillefer *Memoirs*, 218.

vinced that African churches required more than TEE programs, helpful as they were.

In the 1973 AEAM General Assembly, Kato spoke on the subject of "Theological Trends in Africa Today."[22] He emphasized that Africa's greatest need was the training of nationals, not the sending of more missionaries. Thus, as executive director of AEAM's newly created Theological Commission, Kato led its members to plan the launch of the seminary project. No one knew then that more than four years would elapse before FATEB began admitting students in Bangui, and over ten years would pass before the Nairobi Evangelical Graduate School of Theology (NEGST), the anglophone school, would open its doors to students in Nairobi.

The most detailed account of the four years and eight months between the end of the AEAM General Assembly, February 1973, and the beginning of classes in Bangui in October 1977 was written in the memoirs of Eric Maillefer, administrative secretary of AEAM who served from 1971 to 1991.[23] He reported that the first major question concerning the francophone seminary project was its location. Côte d'Ivoire, Chad, and Central African Republic were countries that, to the Theological Commission, seemed best suited for the new school. Church leaders in Côte d'Ivoire were hopeful that Abidjan would be chosen for the seminary. But when British missionary Alastair Kennedy, who had served as French language translator for the General Assembly in Limuru, approached a government minister in Côte d'Ivoire, he found little interest on the part of the minister to assist with the AEAM school proposal. A year earlier in 1972, the Methodists had requested land from a minister of the government to establish a theological seminary. However, their request had been denied. An AEAM application for a theological school in the Côte d'Ivoire received the same negative reply.[24] It is not clear why these requests were denied.

When Kato left the General Assembly in Kenya, he took time to travel to the other two francophone countries under consideration: Chad and the Central African Republic (C.A.R.). He did not yet know whether Kennedy would be successful in Côte d'Ivoire, and though he was anxious to return

---

22. This lecture was published in *Perception* (see Kato, "Theological Trends"). It also appears on a CD compiled by ACTEA, entitled *Byang H. Kato 1936–1975: Perspectives of an African Theologian*. ACTEA is the Association for Christian Theological Education in Africa.

23. Maillefer *Memoirs*, 225–28. See also Breman, *AEA*, 254–55.

24. Alistair Kennedy, letter to Jack Robinson, 10.26.73. For more details, see Alistair Kennedy, letter to Jack Robinson, 2.6.74.

to Texas to complete his doctoral studies,[25] he felt it was important to visit Chad and C.A.R. as soon as possible. In Chad he found the country to be experiencing an African "authenticity" campaign with a strong emphasis on initiation rites. The government campaign there was more anti-Christian than a parallel authenticity movement occurring in Zaire. Discovering the persecution of Christians and the radical Islamic influence of its political leaders, Kato concluded that Chad would be an unwelcoming place to build the new school.

A location somewhere in central Africa seemed desirable, though the travel of students and their families to Bangui from west African countries would be more costly and inconvenient than for those coming from countries in central Africa. After his visit to Chad, Kato stopped in the Central African Republic to talk about the possibility of the theological school with local church leaders. Don Hocking, whom he had met at the General Assembly, was an American Grace Brethren missionary working in C.A.R.'s capital, Bangui. Dr. Isaac Zokoué, C.A.R.'s highly respected Evangelical leader, who had not been able to attend the General Assembly, also made Bangui his primary residence, though he was traveling at the time. Therefore, Don Hocking, with Kato's encouragement, was the one who took the initiative to explore with the C.A.R. government the possibility of locating the francophone school in Bangui.

In June, Hocking wrote to me, as AEAM's francophone secretary for higher education, that he had taken a letter to the minister of education and to the director of national teaching to request permission to establish a theological seminary in Bangui. The government's response was immediate and positive. The national University of Bangui had been founded only four years earlier, in 1969, and developing university level educational programs was a priority of the government. A key question in the mind of Hocking was whether the president of the country would not only approve the founding of an Evangelical seminary in Bangui but might also offer a parcel of land to AEAM for the seminary's construction.[26]

In November 1973, Hocking wrote again saying he had not yet made an official request to the government for land because he wasn't sure how serious Kato was about locating the seminary in Bangui. In early January 1974, Hocking wrote to Kato saying that, even without a formal request for property, the minister of public works, on behalf of the government, was

25. Maillefer, *Memoirs*, 226.
26. Don Hocking, letter to Jack Robinson, 6.10.73.

offering several hectares of land for the seminary near the national University of Bangui. The minister also requested that Kato come to Bangui for a meeting with the president of C.A.R. in late February 1974. However, the minister stipulated that Kato needed to arrive in person and be presented to the minister of education in order to receive a property grant. Hocking wrote, "This is an unbelievable possibility, and we are really rejoicing."[27]

Though the progress toward obtaining land for construction was good news, Dr. Isaac Zokoué doubted that the president would grant land to a foreign organization like AEAM. A C.A.R. Evangelical association of churches was in the process of formation at this time, though not yet officially established. After discussing this concern about a foreign entity receiving property, Zokoué and Hocking decided to ask Kato to agree that, if property were granted, it would be given by the government to the emerging C.A.R. Evangelical association of churches, provided that the association would agree, in turn, to give the property to AEAM to build the school in whatever way its leaders saw fit.[28] The C.A.R. Evangelical church association would thus act as an intermediary between the government and AEAM.

With this in mind, Byang Kato came to Bangui in February 1974 for the meeting with C.A.R.'s former Army general and current national president, Jean-Bédel Bokassa. Kato, Hocking, several local pastors, and Zokoué were present at this audience with the president. Zokoué explained to President Bokassa that the proposed seminary would be sponsored locally by the new Association of Evangelical Churches (AEEC) and that land would be needed.[29] Bokassa had been prepared for this request by his ministers and expressed his desire to have the seminary in C.A.R. Eric Maillefer reported: "Bokassa offered seven acres near the National University, with full access to its library and allowing cultural and academic relations, while giving our school complete autonomy of government and administration, granting of our own degrees."[30] On February 27, 1974, Bokassa signed a decree ordering that the parcel of land be granted for the construction of the graduate school of theology. The gift amounted to three hectares of land (7.4 acres)

27. Don Hocking, letter to Jack Robinson, 11.26.73; Don Hocking, letter to Byang H. Kato, 1.7.74.

28. Don Hocking, letter to Byang H. Kato, 1.7.74.

29. Reference to the Bokassa audience in "Founding of FATEB," 1. The original acronym, AEEC, stood for the Association des Eglises Evangéliques en Centrafrique. Its current name is the Alliance des Eglises Evangéliques en Centrafrique (AEC).

30. Maillefer, *Memoirs*, 226.

and was bordered by two of Bangui's most traveled thoroughfares. The decree stipulated that the school would be open to students from all African countries and from the nearby islands of Madagascar and Mauritius.[31]

Earlier in the week of his visit to Bangui, Kato had met with C.A.R. church leaders and had talked with various local groups. In a meeting with 85 local high school and university students, Kato spoke about the new seminary project. Upon hearing him describe a future university-level theological institution in Bangui, "the group prayed for the project," Kato later wrote. "Before they left the room, one of them suggested, 'Let's give feet to our prayers.' From their limited resources, an amount of about $10 was collected and handed to me in a moving ceremony." Kato reported that he had never seen a group of students in Africa take such immediate action after the presentation of a theological school project on the African continent. He noted that this was the first recorded gift of funds to the seminary that was eventually founded in C.A.R. It came from a group of high school and university students in Bangui.[32]

1974–1975: CONSTRUCTING THE FIRST BUILDING

For the leaders of this francophone seminary project to find themselves owning a choice property site in Bangui only one year after the idea of a graduate theological institution had been proposed at the AEAM General Assembly in Limuru seemed almost miraculous. Formal approval by the AEAM executive committee came a few months later, during the Congress on World Evangelization, held in Lausanne, Switzerland, July 16–25, 1974. At that time, the executive committee of AEAM met to discuss the success of the initiative in C.A.R., listened to Kato's report on his audience with President Bokassa, and, after careful consideration of the proposal and its alternatives, decided to formally accept Bokassa's offer and to build the first AEAM seminary in Bangui. Isaac Zokoué then wrote to President Bokassa to inform him of the decision.[33]

31. C.A.R. Government, "Ordonnance No 74/025, autorisant la création d'une Faculté privée de Théologie," 2.27.74. See also AEAM, "Africa Evangelicals Offered Choice Property," the press release of March 20, 1974.

32. Grace Brethren, "President of the Central African Republic Donates Property to Africa's Evangelicals," March 1974. See also Byang H. Kato, "BEST for Africa," Spring 1975. This was a case for the support of BEST.

33. Breman, *AEA*, 255. Three years later, AEAM's Third General Assembly ratified this decision during its business session in Bouaké, Côte d'Ivoire, July 28 to August 3, 1977.

Once the executive committee had decided to locate the francophone seminary in Bangui, the AEAM Theological Commission charged several individuals to carry out the preparatory work needed for its opening. Dr. Paul White, a missionary with the West Indies Mission (later known as World Team), was assigned to find financing for the project, to recruit professors, and to propose a curriculum. Central African leader Isaac Zokoué, who had earned a doctorate in France, was to work with Grace Brethren missionary Don Hocking. Zokoué would head an action committee to carry out building activities and to coordinate the seminary's launch with the C.A.R. government.[34]

Although AEAM had acquired property in Bangui, much work remained to create a functioning educational institution. The people responsible for converting the vision of this school into reality were severely tested over the following three years. First, the land granted to the school was already inhabited by African families living in dwellings of mud walls and tin roofs. The government insisted that they leave the property, but AEAM was expected to pay for their relocation. Once the inhabitants left the property, the government required that the project leaders begin building the new school within three months. How could planning for the use of space, completion of architectural drawings, obtaining permissions to build, and the raising of necessary financing all be completed in such a short time? Any failure to comply risked difficulty with the municipal authorities. In addition, the question remained of how these African pastors and foreign missionaries, who knew little about managing such projects, could accomplish all this in the C.A.R.[35]

The project leaders realized that someone with professional training and experience was needed to lay out a sensible plan for use of the terrain and to draw up building plans before construction could begin. Jack Dangers, an Evangelical Free Church missionary, was suggested by Don Hocking as someone who might consider assisting with the project in Bangui. Dangers had spent 20 years in northwestern Congo constructing hospital

---

34. Breman, *AEA*, 255. This meeting of the Theological Commission took place in Lausanne, Switzerland, during the Congress that ran from July 16 to 25, 1974. Isaac Zokoué was present at the Congress, though Don Hocking was not. Primary responsibility for the work of the local action committee in Bangui was given to Zokoué, a Central African, to build on the work that Hocking had accomplished for the seminary project over the previous 18 months. See also Don Hocking, letter to Jack Robinson, 8.12.74.

35. René Daidanso, Isaac Zokoué, and Don Hocking, letter to Jack Robinson, Paul White, Tite Tiénou, and Byang H. Kato, 8.31.74.

buildings and schools for the Free Church Mission there. AEAM's administrative secretary, Eric Maillefer, knew Dangers well from his years of service in Congo (Zaire), working under the same mission. Maillefer affirmed that the action committee in Bangui could not find a better person for the job needed in Bangui than Jack Dangers.

I was back in the United States after three years in Bunia, northeastern Zaire, and met with Dangers in late July 1974. As Dangers's furlough was coming to an end, I asked him to consider going to Bangui for a few months, to do the initial planning needed for the seminary. Dangers responded that, if he could get the approval of his mission board and his family, he would be willing to go to C.A.R. for two months. AEAM would need to pay for his flight costs and provide the funds needed in Bangui to accomplish the work. I wrote to Dangers's mission board director, requesting approval for him to undertake this project, told Dangers to plan on going, and informed Kato of his actions. I asked Kato to telegram me only if he did not agree with this plan.[36]

On September 23, Dangers wrote to say that the Evangelical Free Church Mission had given him permission to go to Bangui for an "undetermined period of time." He and his wife planned to arrive in Bangui on October 22, 1974.[37] Kato approved the action committee's budget for Dangers's work.[38] Within the first week after his arrival, the positive impact of Dangers's experience was felt in the project.[39] By the end of December, financial estimates were completed for three professors' houses, five married students' duplexes, three furnished classrooms, a dormitory for six single men, a dining hall, and a kitchen. With costs for a storage shed, tools, pickup truck, and building plans, plus compensation for families that had to vacate the land, a total estimate of $105,500 was made for this initial work of preparing for construction.[40]

Dangers returned to the United States after the beginning of 1975 with his planning work complete and having made a strategic contribution to the construction that followed. His mission had already indicated that he would not remain to do the building.[41] Mr. Al Balzer, a missionary builder

---

36. Jack Robinson, letter to Byang H. Kato, 8.5.74.
37. Jack Dangers, letter to Jack Robinson, 9.23.74.
38. Byang H. Kato, letter to Don Hocking, 10.24.74.
39. Jack Dangers, letter to Jack Robinson, October 1974.
40. Byang H. Kato, rough estimates of initial costs at Bangui, 12.31.74.
41. Robert Dillon, letter to Byang H. Kato, 10.22.74. See also Isaac Zokoué, letter in

with the Grace Brethren in Bangui, agreed to supervise the first phase of the construction, beginning in April 1975.[42] The departure of the last residents on the property occurred in early January, and enough money had been raised to begin building three months later when Al Balzer became available.

In early 1975, the seminary being planned for C.A.R. did not have an official name, though the lack of it did not seem to be a major issue. In a letter that Paul White sent to the francophone members of the AEAM Theological Commission, he devoted two sentences to the name of the seminary. He reported that Zokoué had proposed that the school be called "La Faculté de Théologie Evangélique de Bangui." The acronym "FATEB," by which the school is known today, was not mentioned in the letter. White endorsed the proposal and added that the French name could be translated into English as the Evangelical Seminary of Bangui and could be used in the school's publicity and correspondence.[43] At the same time, during Kato's visit to the United States, he and I discussed a slightly different name for the school in English: the "Bangui Evangelical School of Theology." Soon, English speakers began to call it by its acronym, "BEST."

With Al Balzer scheduled to get construction under way in April 1975, the action committee decided to plan a public cornerstone laying in Bangui on May 4, 1975. Local television and Radio Bangui agreed to provide media coverage. Electricity and water lines had been connected. Stationery was being printed for newsletters. The president of AEAM, Samuel Odunaike of Nigeria, agreed to come as the special speaker for the occasion. In addition, a week of evangelistic meetings was scheduled around this event. At this point, estimates for the cost of all the buildings needed for FATEB were running around a half million US dollars. A public event of laying the cornerstone was needed not only to provide visibility and good will in the capital city but also to attract the interest of prospective donors to fund the project.[44]

On May 4, 1975, over a thousand people gathered for the cornerstone-laying ceremony. Six choirs from Bangui churches sang at the celebration. Pastor Jean Jacques Nimézéambi, a subsequent member of FATEB's board

French to Paul White, February 1975.

42. Isaac Zokoué, letter in French to Paul White, February 1975.

43. Paul White, letter to Byang H. Kato and the Theological Commission (francophone), 3.8.75.

44. Don Hocking, letter to Jack Robinson, 4.14.75.

and eventually a FATEB graduate, explained in French why Bangui was chosen for the seminary. Brethren Pastor Pounoukoussara spoke in the local language of Sango. Television and radio technicians recorded and later broadcast the entire event as each member of the action committee laid a stone in the foundation of the first building. AEAM President Odunaike presided over the ceremony, and various individuals and churches contributed financially to the project. FATEB had made an excellent beginning in the eyes of the citizens of Bangui.[45]

Lack of adequate funding for building the school remained a tremendous obstacle. From mid-1974 to mid-1975 enough money was raised to make a good start on the construction. But by the end of August 1975, most of the funds had been spent. Hocking wrote, "We are in financial trouble. I only have a few thousand francs left (no, I didn't say dollars). In fact, I think we only have about $400.00 or so left. Al [Balzer] still has . . . $10,000.00 but that will go in a hurry. Inflation is killing us. Plus, there were a lot of hidden costs that were not figured into the budget." Hocking went on to give details.[46] Milton Baker, at the Conservative Baptist Mission headquarters, asked a colleague to produce 20,000 copies of a promotional brochure for the school.[47] Students at Trinity Evangelical Divinity School in the US raised $5,000. The two large mission associations in the United States, EFMA and IFMA, were supportive and assisted in informing their francophone missionaries. In 1974–1975, approximately $60,000 was received.[48]

1975–1976: DESIGNING THE SEMINARY CURRICULUM

The Theological Commission of AEAM met in Bangui July 7–10, 1975, along with the local action committee. Isaac Zokoué was present for this important meeting, though in April he had returned to his residence in Abidjan, where he was serving as the traveling secretary for francophone Africa's InterVarsity groups (GBU, Groupes Bibliques Universitaires). Don Hocking had replaced him as head of the action committee while Dr. Paul White maintained overall responsibility for the seminary project in Bangui.[49] Dr. John Winston, president of the Evangelical seminary at Vaux-

---

45. AEAM, "Report of FATEB cornerstone laying ceremony," 1, August 1975.
46. Don Hocking, letter to Jack Robinson, 8.31.75.
47. Milton Baker, letter to Jack Robinson and the heads of EFMA and IFMA, 10.6.75.
48. Don Hocking, letter to John Zielasko, Grace Brethren Mission, 10.14.75.
49. Paul White, newsletter, 10.20.75, asking recipients to serve on the FATEB General

sur-Seine in France (Faculté Libre de Théologie Evangélique), attended these July meetings in Bangui. Most Evangelical French-speaking Africans who wanted university-level theological training had been attending Vaux, and John Winston was supportive of the francophone seminary project in C.A.R. This was his first visit to Africa, and it proved to be instructive for him. He also gave the members of the Theological Commission wise counsel on how to move ahead.[50] The meeting did not solve the financial crisis, but it injected optimism and realism into the minds of the project leaders.

The members of the Theological Commission who gathered in July 1975 for four days in Bangui included eight Africans and three Americans. FATEB, as an educational institution, not just as buildings on a campus, began taking definite shape during that meeting. A draft constitution and by-laws for the school were written. Professors' salaries, student tuition levels, financial aid, admission requirements, and length of the academic program were discussed, and proposals were made. Under the authority of the AEAM executive committee, AEAM's Theological Commission would remain FATEB's highest authority. A FATEB General Assembly, with wide representation throughout francophone Africa, was also designed, and the names of 39 delegates were suggested, mostly from African countries. FATEB's General Assembly would meet once every three or four years at the same time as the AEAM General Assembly, and it would be accountable to the AEAM Theological Commission. A FATEB board of governors of seven members, mostly local individuals, was proposed that would provide direct oversight of the seminary in Bangui. The doyen (administrative head of the institution) of FATEB would be accountable to the board of governors which, in turn, would function under the authority of the FATEB General Assembly. The members of the board of governors would be members of the General Assembly as well, but they would meet in Bangui more frequently, at least once a year. The board of governors held its first meeting from December 29, 1975, to January 1, 1976. The board discussed campus development issues with the builder, Al Balzer. The board also agreed upon strategies for student recruitment and plans for the completion of funding for the school.[51]

Assembly.

50. Paul White, letters to members of the AEA Theological Commission, 4.25.75 and 6.5.75. See Paul White, letter to Jack Robinson (with Kato photo), 7.22.75.

51. AEAM, Minutes [Procès-verbal] in French, of the Theological Commission (francophone section) and Action Committee in Bangui, 7.7–10.75; White was president of the meeting; Tiénou was secretary.

An African Dream

In September 1975, Paul White met with Byang Kato in London to discuss progress. The target date for opening the school was 1976, just a year away, but White was already considering a delay until 1977 so that the preparation of buildings, library, curriculum, and professors could be more firmly in place. In the London meeting, Kato proposed that White be named doyen of the school.[52] With this support from Kato, and with assurance that the authority for work on the project continued to rest with AEAM's Theological Commission, White began planning with a clearer sense of direction.

In October 1975, White drew up a list of questions still to be resolved. These were the issues that required solutions if the school was to become a credible, durable educational institution. The members of the action committee, the Theological Commission, and especially White and Hocking had to wrestle with these problems to launch the school. The July 1975 meeting had put propositions on the table, but decisions needed to be made. These included legal issues like ownership of the seminary, constitution, and government agreements properly documented. Financial questions both for capital investment as well as for operations were challenging. Administration of the school required a board of governors, bylaws, and personnel decisions to be approved. The academic concerns included instructional personnel appointments, institutional objectives, program, curriculum, degrees, accreditation, and academic standards. Student affairs included questions of student recruitment, provision of student financial aid, and assistance with the placement of graduates after the completion of their studies. Theological commitments of the seminary touched on questions of cooperation with other groups and their doctrinal distinctives. Public relations and the promotion of FATEB also presented challenges. Developing a library and various learning resources was critical. Engaging students in practical field work required local opportunities to be identified. All these questions constituted a mountain of tasks for a tiny group of people to carry out in addition to their oversight of campus building construction.[53]

Leaders of Christian organizations in French-speaking Africa raised critical questions about the seminary project, including Hocking's own Grace Brethren Mission director, John Zielasko. He wanted to know who oversaw the seminary. Was it a stand-alone institution, or was it under the

---

52. Paul White, letter to Jack Robinson, 9.17.75.

53. Milton Baker, letter to Byang H. Kato (with attached list of problems to be resolved), 10.6.75.

authority of some other organizational entity? In mid-1975 a meeting of the executive committee of AEAM had taken place in Lagos, Nigeria. By then, the constitution of the seminary had been drafted, and a statute was added stating unequivocally that the operation of the seminary was "under the jurisdiction of AEAM." AEAM's authority over FATEB, over its General Assembly and its board of governors, would be exercised through the AEAM Theological Commission.[54]

From November 21 to 26, 1975, AEAM held a Theological Conference in Nairobi bringing together both the francophone and anglophone members of AEAM's Theological Commission. It included representatives of 13 African theological schools and several European and American observers. In addition to hosting the presentation of theological papers and discussions of current theological issues, the Theological Commission met to talk about the future of the two AEAM graduate schools in both anglophone and francophone Africa. The most significant issue for FATEB was the decision to postpone the opening of the school in Bangui from 1976 to 1977. Three issues contributed to this delay. White could not arrive in time to make final preparations for the school opening. Hocking, who was slated to teach, would go on furlough in 1976. The library needed to acquire more books and periodicals before classes began. This year-long delay would also give additional time to complete necessary funding and building construction essential to the program.[55]

In January 1976, White wrote a report distributed to the Evangelical mission organizations working in francophone Africa. It was the most comprehensive account of progress to date, progress that was the result of three years of work by many individuals and organizations. White reported on the November 1975 executive committee's adoption of a constitution and by-laws for FATEB, the ratification of FATEB's governance structure, with a General Assembly of 40 approved members, and a board of governors with seven confirmed members. In its first meeting, White reported, the governing board made the following decisions: (1) The opening of FATEB would be scheduled for October, 1977; (2) With the adoption of a curriculum and university level entrance requirements established, FATEB would offer a five-year program of study, leading to the equivalent of a master of divinity

54. Don Hocking, letter to John Zielasko, Grace Brethren Mission, 10.14.75. Copies were sent to Edwin Frizen, Wade Coggins, Jack Robinson, Byang H. Kato, and Paul White.

55. AEAM, Theological Conference, Theological Commission and minutes, 11.21–26.1975. Opening of FATEB postponed from 1976 to 1977, 9.

degree; (3) Dr. White would move with his family to Bangui in September 1976 to prepare for the opening of the school a year later; (4) Tuition, room, board, and meals would cost $1,000 for single students and $1,300 for married students; (5) FATEB would become a high level theological research center, to provide solid biblical answers to Africa's specific problems, thus strengthening the Evangelical church in francophone Africa; (6) FATEB would aim to be a living and vital part of the churches' activity, engaged in the daily reality of the churches' life, refusing to become a theological "ivory tower."[56] White also reported 25 written requests from prospective students about studying at the school. In addition, $75,000 had been received for the seminary project. To open the school in 1977, another $125,000 would be necessary.

Though most of this was good news for FATEB, one issue created immense pain for those associated with AEAM and with the seminary project in Bangui. Just a month after the November 1975 Theological Conference, Dr. Byang Kato died suddenly, December 19, 1975, on the shores of the Kenyan coast near Mombasa. Kato had served as AEAM's general secretary for almost three years. As head of its Theological Commission, he had spearheaded the effort to establish the graduate school of theology in Bangui, while assisting the anglophones with their seminary project as well. In addition, he had become the friend and colleague of those most closely associated with these projects.

Kato was taking a vacation break with his family on the spectacular east African shore bordering the Indian Ocean. At midday, three days after their arrival, Kato's two boys left the beach and headed back to their cottage, leaving Kato alone on the shore. Kato failed to join the boys for lunch. When the family went looking for him, he had disappeared. A day later his body was found on the beach where they had been swimming. The cause of his death remains a mystery. Byang Kato's tragic death at age 39 shocked the Evangelical world, not just in Africa but around the globe. Bruce J. Nicholls wrote, "Byang was a twentieth century prophet, somewhat in the school of an earlier African, Tertullian, for while he identified with black Africa in its cry for liberation against unjust oppression, he was fearless in his denunciation of all liberal theology and philosophy that deviated from the authority of the Bible as the Word of God."[57]

---

56. Paul White, letter to missions with work in francophone Africa, 1.23.76.

57. Breman, *AEA*, 49.

Vision of a Training Institution—Byang Kato

Personal descriptions of Byang Kato's life over his tenure of almost three years as general secretary of AEAM are recorded in the *Memoirs* of his administrative secretary, Eric Maillefer.[58] Though Kato's sudden departure was a terrible setback for AEAM, Maillefer was convinced that the association had been well established. Maillefer had been involved with AEAM since it was founded almost 11 years earlier in 1965. "If it had managed to get this far," Maillefer mused, "why could it not survive further till another African leader could be found?" And it did continue until Kato's successor was chosen a year and a half later in 1977 at AEAM's Third General Assembly in Bouaké, Côte d'Ivoire.[59]

---

58. Maillefer, *Memoirs*, 218–19; 224–26; 229–30; 238–40. See also Breman, *AEA*, 40–53; 384–400; 429–36; 532–43.

59. Maillefer, *Memoirs*, 240.

CHAPTER 3

First Years of Classes—Paul White

1976-1977: APPOINTING FATEB'S FIRST DOYEN

AT THE NEXT MEETING of the AEAM executive committee, March 15–19, 1976, a Byang Kato Memorial Fund was established to assist with the "promotion, encouragement and provision of higher theological training and education of Evangelical Africans within an African context."[1] The executive committee then focused the rest of its business on steps that Kato would have supported. They reorganized the Theological Commission that Kato had led, established the Evangelical Accrediting Association of Africa (later called the Association for Christian Theological Education in Africa, ACTEA), formed an Evangelical Theological Society of Africa, and continued planning for the two emerging graduate schools of theology. Recommendations from the Theological Commission's November 1975 meeting and from the board of governors meeting December 29, 1975, to January 1, 1976, were, in general, approved. The local action committee was dissolved and replaced by FATEB's new board of governors: Chairman Paul White; Vice-Chairman Don Hocking; Secretary Isaac Zokoué. Dr. Paul White was also proposed as doyen of FATEB. The opening of the seminary was set for October 15, 1977. The FATEB constitution and by-laws were revised to clarify the relationship of the seminary to AEAM.[2] Finally, the word "inerrant" was inserted into FATEB's confession of faith, article 1, that

---

1. AEAM, minutes of executive committee, French and English versions, 3.15–19.76.
2. AEAM, minutes of executive committee, 3.15–19.76.

dealt with biblical authority. Otherwise, the confession of faith was identical with that of AEAM.[1]

With the designation of Dr. Paul White as doyen (president) of FATEB and with a board of governors that had begun to function, the management of the seminary project shifted away from three years of guidance by committees to the personal leadership of Dr. White as doyen who was accountable to FATEB's board of governors. White's communication in July of 1976 to the members of FATEB's General Assembly, which included all the members of the board of governors, reflected this change in the management of the seminary under White's direction.[2] White had planned to move his family to Bangui in 1976, but the shortage of funds needed to continue campus building construction persuaded him to spend the 1976–1977 academic year in the USA in fundraising.[3] At the same time, White was making appointments for faculty and staff in preparation for the opening of the school.

During their 1976–1977 year of residence in America, White moved his family to Trinity Evangelical Divinity School in Deerfield, Illinois, where he also taught several courses in New Testament and missions. White's wife, Arline, had earlier given birth to a succession of four daughters, and in March 1977, a son. In April, a month later, White began an intensive series of fundraising visits in North America, Europe, and Africa. At the same time, he continued to communicate with prospective students about FATEB's formal opening in October 1977. The number of applicants had reached 59 by mid-1977.[4]

1977–1978: BEGINNING OF SEMINARY CLASSES

On his way to Bangui, White flew to the Côte d'Ivoire for the Third General Assembly of AEAM, July 30 to August 2, 1977, held in the city of Bouaké. More than 300 participants from Africa, Europe, and North America

---

1. AEAM, minutes of executive committee, 3.15–19.76. See also Maillefer, *Memoirs*, 227. Maillefer explains the background of this addition to the FATEB confession of faith requested by the board of governors, influenced by the Grace Brethren Mission operating in C.A.R.

2. Paul White, letter to members of the FATEB General Assembly, 7.20.76.

3. Paul White, letter to members of the FATEB General Assembly, 7.20.76. See also Paul White, newsletter, November 1976, to friends, in French.

4. See Paul White, letters to students, 1.27.77, 7.1.77, and 7.8.77, in French.

gathered for this continental meeting of Evangelicals. The delegates included 175 Africans from 32 African countries and 130 expatriates, with 123 organizations represented. Tokunboh Adeyemo of Nigeria was elected general secretary to replace Byang Kato, who had died 18 months earlier. Nigerian AEAM President Odunaike requested that a memorial service be conducted in honor of Kato. His widow was in attendance. Tite Tiénou of Upper Volta (later named Burkina Faso), a graduate of the Evangelical seminary at Vaux-sur-Seine in France (Faculté Libre de Théologie Evangélique), was named executive secretary of the Theological Commission.[5]

Concluding his service as interim executive director of the Theological Commission since Kato's death, White made a report to the AEAM General Assembly in which he announced that about 30 students would be enrolled for the beginning of classes at FATEB in October. He also reported that the initial phase of the campus construction program was virtually complete. It included a single-story building that would have space for a classroom and faculty offices. Funding was needed for the next phase, which included the construction of a two-story building for multiple classrooms and administrative offices.[6]

The cadre of professors already recruited included Don Hocking of the Grace Brethren Mission. He had returned to Bangui from a study leave in the USA, obtaining a doctorate in theology. Floyd Shank, an experienced professor and theological school director in Gabon, also joined the faculty. In addition to his administrative responsibilities, Paul White accepted a teaching load.[7] Nineteen students obtained the funding needed to enroll in FATEB: one from Chad, one from Guinea, eight from Zaire, and nine from C.A.R., a group comprising twelve married students and seven single men. One of the full-time students was a married woman. The oldest student was 37 years old, the father of three children, and a former police officer in Kinshasa. He gained the respect of the other students and became their informal leader.

After several weeks of classes, the main student complaints were the weight of their work and the amount of time spent in library research. White explained to them that this academic pressure required the kind of

---

5. Paul White, newsletter, 12.6.77. See also Maillefer, *Memoirs*, 243–47; Breman, *AEA*, 70–74.

6. AEAM, minutes of the Third General Assembly, 7.30–8.2.77, business sessions.

7. AEAM, minutes of the Third General Assembly, 7.30–8.2.77, business sessions.

discipline they as students needed to prepare them to serve the Lord.⁸ In a message to the board of governors, White explained that the students spent 18 hours a week in classes but that FATEB's educational philosophy also put a strong emphasis on research. Hence, considerable time in the library was necessary.⁹

The library, ultimately named the Byang Kato Memorial Library, opened with 1,600 books on its shelves. White hoped that it would one day become the best theological library in francophone Africa. In addition to the building needed for classes and offices, a residence for single students was also included in the second phase of construction plans. The total cost of this phase was estimated at nearly $200,000, of which only $20,000 was on hand.¹⁰ Students also faced steep financial challenges. The cost of their education at FATEB exceeded the resources of virtually all the applicants. Help from their churches was important, but most churches could not easily bear the costs of sending a student to FATEB. Thus, economic challenges were substantial both for the students and for the new seminary.

As classes began in October of 1977, almost five years had passed since the conception of FATEB in Limuru, Kenya, at the Second General Assembly of the Association of Evangelicals in Africa. A resume of those years includes the following events:

- 1973: AEAM decided to create the first university level Evangelical seminary in French Africa.
- 1974: Land for the new school was granted in Bangui by C.A.R's president.
- 1975: Ground was broken on campus, and the cornerstone was laid for the first building.
- 1976: FATEB's first doyen was appointed, and preparations were made for opening classes.
- 1977: AEAM approved the admission of students for the first academic year in October of 1977.

---

8. Paul White, communiqué to the FATEB board of governors, 12.2.77, in French. White wrote this newsletter during a few days of vacation, prompted by the coronation of Jean-Bédel Bokassa as emperor of Central Africa on 12.4.77. The imperial parade passed down the avenue in front of FATEB on its way to the sports arena where the ceremony took place.

9. Paul White, communiqué to the FATEB board of governors, 12.2.77, in French.

10. [No name, but clearly by Paul White], B.E.S.T. Information, 11.1.77, in English.

Moving from a dream of this magnitude to its realization in less than five years seemed to some people like a miracle. The future path would not be easy, but the journey had begun well and would not be abandoned.

Pressures of another sort were mounting in FATEB's first year of operation that would be even more difficult to manage than the shortage of funds. During the first year of classes, which began in October 1977, the students identified an issue in early 1978 that would test the stability of FATEB to its limits. In a message to FATEB's administration, the students said that they "regretted very bitterly that the President of the Board of Governors had put two leaders . . . at the head of FATEB."[11] Their letter went on to note that faculty member Don Hocking was functioning not only as a professor of the seminary but was also serving as vice-president of the board of governors under its president, Isaac Zokoué. However, with the frequent absence of Zokoué on his travels for the GBU, the students reported that Hocking saw himself as authorized to intervene in the administrative affairs of FATEB, and to do so without conferring with the doyen. Hocking had told the students that the Association of Evangelical Churches in Central Africa (AEEC) was the permanent representative of AEAM in the country. This was not true. The AEEC was indeed a member of AEAM but had not been given any part in AEAM's oversight of the school. The students saw Hocking using his influence, as a member of the AEEC board, to exert his own authority over the business of the school in opposition to the formally established leadership of White. The students made explicit in their letter the ways in which this situation affected them. The tensions that had been growing between Hocking and White also become visible to the campus community.

On March 28, 1978, Isaac Zokoué, president of the board of governors, sent a letter to the 40 members of FATEB's General Assembly in which he referred to the "deep division" that existed between the two leaders. In addition, he wrote that Doyen White had declined to commit to serving a second academic year because of this tense situation. The conflict had grown so acute and intractable by late March that Zokoué could see only two alternatives: either to close the seminary for an indeterminate period or to request White to leave FATEB at the end of the academic year. He requested the members of the General Assembly to send him their vote by

---

11. Students of FATEB, letter to FATEB board of governors, 3.25.78; Breman, *AEA*, 255. In 1977, Zokoué had been named president of the board of governors, replacing White, at the Third AEAM General Assembly, Bouaké, 7.30–8.2.77.

telegram on whether the board should accept the first alternative, accept the second, reject both, or abstain from voting.[12]

The board of the Association of Evangelical Churches in Central Africa met on March 30, 1978, to discuss the problems at FATEB. Two members of their board served on FATEB's board of governors, and both saw the doyen as the cause of the conflict. The AEEC board decided that if the AEAM executive committee did not act, the AEEC would withdraw from AEAM, and two of their members, Pierre Yougouda and Don Hocking, would also withdraw from FATEB's board of governors. The AEEC also expressed hope that, in such a case, AEAM would ask Paul White to resign from FATEB.[13]

The AEEC president, Doko-Manga, wrote a letter to the head of AEAM's executive committee requesting that White be replaced as doyen of FATEB. He mentioned three reasons why the AEEC considered his leadership unacceptable: (1) He had admitted non-Evangelical students to FATEB; (2) He was conducting weekly communion services on campus, twice using wine in the communion cups; (3) He had participated in an ecumenical event outside of FATEB. The AEEC president saw these as the reasons why Hocking had decided to resign from FATEB as professor. Under such circumstances as he described, Doko-Manga felt it impossible for the AEEC to collaborate with the doyen.[14]

AEAM's president, Samuel Odunaike, wrote three letters on April 8 to resolve the crisis at FATEB. One letter went to the president of the AEEC, one to Isaac Zokoué, president of the board of governors, and one to Paul White, FATEB's doyen.[15] The AEAM executive committee had met in Nairobi April 5–7, and Odunaike's letters reflected the committee's consensus. Odunaike reminded the AEEC president that the relationship of the AEEC association of churches to AEAM was unrelated to FATEB and that the AEEC relationship to AEAM should not have been called into question because of perceived problems with FATEB. He also indicated that FATEB was under the direct authority of its board of governors, and that the board

---

12. Isaac Zokoué, letter to FATEB General Assembly, 3.28.78.

13. AEC, minutes of the AEC board meeting (to address the conflict at FATEB between Hocking and White), 3.30.78. At this time the AEC (*Alliance Evangélique en Centrafrique*) was known as AEEC (*Association des Eglises Evangéliques en Centrafrique*).

14. Doko-Manga, letter to the president of the executive committee of AEAM, 3.30.78.

15. Samuel Odunaike, letter to Doko-Manga, president of AEC, 4.8.78; Samuel Odunaike, letter to Isaac Zokoué, president of FATEB board of Governors, 4.8.78; Samuel Odunaike, letter to Paul White, doyen of FATEB, 4.8.78.

of governors was the body charged with resolving issues with the seminary's daily operations, not the AEAM executive committee to which the AEEC president had written. However, Odunaike offered to have either the president or the general secretary of AEAM visit Bangui to serve as a mediator, to resolve the conflict there.

In his letter to Isaac Zokoué, Odunaike agreed with the way the board of governors had dealt with the three issues raised by the AEEC president. Only Evangelical students should be admitted to FATEB. No more communion services were to be held on FATEB's campus. Ecumenical encounters by faculty members would occur only in their personal capacities, not as representatives of FATEB. (Odunaike's opinion on these issues was challenged by subsequent doyens.) Odunaike also assured Zokoué that (1) personally, he did not want to see White leave FATEB; (2) the executive committee would not interfere with the work of FATEB's board of governors; and (3) he would try to send a mediatorial representative of AEAM to Bangui to assist in resolving the crisis.

To Paul White, Odunaike indicated that (1) FATEB's situation was under the direct authority of the FATEB board of governors, that (2) he would attempt to send mediatorial assistance to Bangui on behalf of AEAM, and that (3) he prayed for wisdom and grace for the doyen as he worked to resolve this problem.

On April 19, Don Hocking's American supervisor, John Zielasko, general director of the Foreign Missionary Society of the Brethren Church (USA), known informally as the Grace Brethren, wrote to Dr. White to ask for explanations of the three issues that the AEEC said had led to Hocking's resignation from the FATEB faculty. He also added a fourth question about whether FATEB was encouraging students to speak in tongues.[16] In a three-page letter White responded to these issues. The AEEC and Hocking had raised these issues because they believed they represented non-Evangelical beliefs and actions on the part of the doyen.[17] In his reply, White wrote in detail about his theological positions regarding the questions raised, how the accusations of his practice misrepresented the truth, and how he had dealt with these issues. He also affirmed that these concerns were secondary to the real reason for Hocking's resignation, though he did not elaborate on that point in his reply to Zielasko. He further stated his continuing

---

16. John Zielasko, letter to Paul White (raising questions about some of White theological beliefs and actions as doyen), 4.19.78.

17. Paul White, letter to John Zielasko, 5.9.78.

commitment to submit to the authority of the FATEB board of governors in all aspects of his leadership of the seminary.

On June 11, 1978, FATEB held an official ceremony marking the close of its first academic year. The students and their families participated in the celebration. Songs and recitations marked the event. A student from each of the four countries represented in the student body recounted his appreciation for God's grace during his first year of theological studies. A large group of pastors and friends joined the campus community on this special occasion.[18]

Among the reasons for joy at year's end were the experiences of the 12 married students and their families. They had arrived in October with a combined total of 19 children. By June, six new infants had increased that number to twenty-five. In keeping with an African tradition that sometimes leads parents to name a newborn after a circumstance associated with the child's birth, the couple who welcomed the first of the babies born that year promptly named him Fateb One.[19] Besides the joy of family additions, gratitude was expressed for the work of Paul White's wife, Arline, who directed a practical learning program on biblical and social topics for the student wives not enrolled in the degree program. She contributed to the education of the preschool children as well.[20]

1978–1979: CONFRONTING LEADERSHIP CONFLICT

After the first-year closing ceremonies on June 11, 1978, Floyd Shank decided to communicate to Paul White his evaluation of the doyen's leadership. Shank was the other professor, besides White, who had taught at FATEB throughout the first academic year. He wrote about many concerns that he described in a long letter to White.[21] Shank presented eight issues in his document, noting that some of his concerns were shared by Hocking as well, though Hocking had already resigned. On the morning of June 17, 1978, Shank hand-carried his letter to White, who asked to meet with

---

18. Paul White, newsletter to friends and supporters, 6.15.78.

19. Paul White, FATEB Information Bulletin no. 3, to friends and supporters of FATEB, July 1978.

20. Students FATEB (from Zaire), letter to Dirindo Marini-Bodho, reporting on their year at FATEB, 8.2.78.

21. Floyd Shank, letter to Paul White (regarding eight concerns he had about White's leadership of FATEB), 6.16.78.

him later in the day. Shank agreed but asked that Hocking also be present. White declined to invite Hocking to join them. White talked about the letter for half an hour while Shank listened. At the conclusion of the interview, they both prayed. Shank then asked for a meeting in which Hocking would be present, but White would not agree to such a meeting.

After returning to the USA, Shank sent a copy of the letter he had given to White to the members of the FATEB board of governors and to AEAM President Odunaike. In an accompanying cover letter, Shank said that White did not acknowledge the validity of any of the eight points that he had raised. Shank also said that he would respect whatever decisions the board of governors and President Odunaike reached regarding his concerns about the doyen's relationship with the AEAM and with his faculty members. Shank expressed the hope that solutions would be found that would help FATEB both in the present and in its future years. At the same time, he indicated that his work at FATEB was finished.[22]

With considerable uncertainty about what would happen to FATEB because of these relational problems, Isaac Zokoué, as president of the board of governors, held a board meeting July 28–29, 1978. Three decisions were made at that time by the board: (1) to ask White to cease his responsibilities as doyen of FATEB but not as professor; (2) to ask Hocking to resume his duties as professor at FATEB (negative student evaluations of his teaching had precipitated his resignation in March 1978); (3) to announce to both White and Hocking that they were suspended from the board of governors as of July 29, 1978. In addition, the board invited Tite Tiénou to become doyen of FATEB.[23]

On July 31, White wrote a lengthy letter to the 40 members of the General Assembly of FATEB who had been sent a copy of the three decisions made by the board of governors, including his own dismissal as doyen. In his letter White contested the way the decision of the board of governors had been made to release him as doyen. White argued that it failed to respect the process for such action outlined in article 17 of the FATEB constitution and article B of its by-laws. In addition, White reported on the reaction of the students when they were told that the board had voted to request Hocking to return to FATEB as a member of the faculty. In a meeting

---

22. Floyd Shank, cover letter to the FATEB board of governors and president of AEAM (containing his 6.16.78 letter to Paul White), 6.23.78.

23. Isaac Zokoué, letter to Harold Alexander, director of overseas ministries, Worldteam (with a copy to Paul White), 7.29.78. This was White's mission organization.

with Tite Tiénou, who was a member of the board of governors, and with White, the students expressed their categorical refusal to take courses taught by Hocking, giving two reasons, as reported by White: Hocking's incompetence to teach at a university level and the quality of his spiritual life that contributed no edification to their own spiritual formation.[24]

White, having been suspended from the board of governors and requested by it to function only as a FATEB professor, no longer as doyen, nevertheless wrote to the FATEB General Assembly, suggesting two options on which he asked the members to vote and to send their choices to governing board President Zokoué. (1) White remains doyen; Hocking does not return as professor; Tiénou joins the faculty as professor. (2) Tiénou becomes doyen; White remains as professor; Don Muchmore, missionary with the Unevangelized Fields Mission and former professor at the Evangelical theological school in Bunia, Zaire, joins the faculty as professor; Hocking does not return as professor.[25] In the two alternatives he suggested, White expressed his willingness to step out of his role as doyen in the second option, but in neither option did he accept the reinstatement of Hocking to the faculty as a professor.

A month later, at the end of August 1978, Isaac Zokoué, president of the board of governors, proposed that the board assume the leadership of FATEB instead of the doyen. He went on in his letter to assign responsibilities to three men: Paul White, academic director; Don Muchmore, administrative director; Don Hocking, responsible for finance, construction, and government relations. All three would, in addition, serve as professors.[26] This proposition was never carried out because before the new academic year 1978–1979 began, Don Hocking left Bangui for the town of Bata in the interior of C.A.R., to establish a separate seminary there for the Grace Brethren. Don Muchmore refused to join FATEB's faculty until the conflict between Hocking and White was resolved. In the end, Muchmore chose to join Hocking and teach in Bata at the new Brethren seminary there.[27]

By late August 1978, White realized that both the president of the AEEC, Doko-Manga, and Dr. Floyd Shank had written letters to FATEB's General Assembly members that contained multiple accusations. White felt he needed to defend his actions and correct misrepresentations of his

---

24. Paul White, letter to members of the FATEB General Assembly, 7.31.78.
25. Paul White, letter to members of the FATEB General Assembly, 7.31.78.
26. Isaac Zokoué, proposal for resolving conflicts within FATEB, 8.31.78.
27. Isaac Zokoué, "Founding of FATEB," 2.

positions and decisions. In his own lengthy letter to the General Assembly, White answered their negative comments point by point.[28] Two weeks later White began a general message to his friends with the words, "We've just come through what is probably the most massive attack on our ministry that we have ever experienced."[29] White went on to write that the president of AEAM, Samuel Odunaike, had come to Bangui in July of 1978 in an attempt to understand the underlying causes of the conflict. By the end of his visit, Odunaike, as president of AEAM, had decided to continue supporting White as doyen. Even though this left White as the only professor remaining at the seminary, White reported that the students were pleased with this outcome and that he and his family were grateful to be able to continue their ministry there.

In FATEB's December 1978 Information Bulletin, White reported on the beginning of the seminary's second year of training. Sixteen students had completed the first academic year and were joined by seventeen new students as the second year began. Eleven were from C.A.R., nineteen from Zaire, one from Chad, one from Guinea, and one from Uganda. Twenty-one of the thirty-three were married. Fifty-three children, twelve years or younger, lived with their student parents on campus. Programs for student wives and children continued, with assistance by women from city churches. White was still the only resident professor, teaching five courses, but visiting professors were coming from Africa and Europe to share the teaching load. White also had an excellent bilingual secretary, Madame Annie, whose help was significant. The library had grown to 4,000 volumes, and lights in the library often enabled students to do research until midnight.[30]

At the end of December 1978, the board of governors met over a four-day period to consider a long agenda of issues. Board member Pierre Yougouda had traveled to Upper Volta (Burkina Faso) to ask the Christian and Missionary Alliance denomination there to release Tite Tiénou to FATEB, to serve as doyen. However, that church did not respond positively to this request. Even so, the board voted to invite Tiénou to serve as doyen for one or two years, to ask American missionary Don Muchmore to head the administration, to request White to serve as academic secretary, and to ask all three men to teach as well. Muchmore declined, and although Tiénou

---

28. Paul White, letter to the FATEB General Assembly (defending himself against his critics), 8.23.78.

29. Paul White, letter to friends, 9.9.78.

30. Paul White, FATEB Information Bulletin no. 4, December 1978.

and White did accept this decision, Tiénou was not released by his church. Thus, White, in addition to his academic role, continued to function as doyen of FATEB during the entire second school year. Along with decisions on these major personnel issues, the board of governors approved plans to construct a multi-story administrative and classroom building, and the search for a competent builder continued.[31]

In February 1979, a Central African contractor agreed to oversee work on the three-story administrative building. Construction began despite delays due to the lack of cement available in the city. The library had acquired another 2,000 books, bringing the total to 6,000. Throughout the second year, students served in various city churches. The local language of Sango was the traditional language of the churches, but the students had started French services in many of the parishes. They also led Bible studies in city churches and schools. Some spoke at university student meetings and encouraged Christians in their faith. White believed that all this ministry activity offered the students practical ways to translate what they were learning in seminary classrooms into practice that served the larger community.[32]

By May of 1979, all 33 students were still enrolled as FATEB was completing its second academic year. White was the only full-time resident professor on campus. In a communication to those who were supporting the seminary with gifts and prayers, he described the results of FATEB's second school year and its prospects for the future. His biggest encouragement was the arrival on May 7 of a Congolese professor, Nzash Luméya, who had studied at the Vaux-sur-Seine seminary in France (Faculté Libre de Théologie Évangélique). Luméya had been serving as the Protestant campus pastor at the University of Zaire in Kinshasa. Teaching both theology and New Testament Greek during the last few weeks of the school year, Luméya expressed his willingness to join the faculty as a resident professor for FATEB's third academic year.[33]

White and his wife, Arline, were dedicated to creating learning opportunities for all the family members of the students. The more than 50 campus children were divided by age into Chicks, Gazelles, and Elephants for educational purposes. Their mothers had access to two sewing machines and received practical instruction in sewing, family management, and

---

31. FATEB, Minutes of the board of governors meeting, Bangui, 12.29.78–1.1.79.
32. Paul White, FATEB Information Bulletin no. 5, May 1979.
33. Paul White, FATEB Information Bulletin no. 5, May 1979.

biblical knowledge. Arline White supervised these activities. In his May 1979 Information Bulletin, the doyen expressed thanks to FATEB's supporters and gratitude to God for the many blessings of the second school year.[34]

In a letter to their personal friends, Arline White offered her perspective on their first two years of life in Bangui. She began by writing, "I have to admit that Africa has won our hearts."[35] Mrs. White wrote of the work her 19-year-old daughter was doing to bring order into the 6,000-book library. She also explained what their 14- and 12-year-old daughters had done in creating a library for the children of the students. She spoke of her work in the school for the children, for their mothers, and in the support of her husband.

> Our load is impossible. Paul works 70 to 80 hours a week. But what tires us out the most are the criticisms and the accusations of other people. De Gaulle once said that it is almost impossible to lead a country of more than 300 sorts of cheese. Is it impossible to found an interdenominational and authentically African seminary, with students from 12 denominations, supported by donors from a multitude of Evangelical contexts, scattered over three different continents? There are groups in many places that want to express their views about FATEB. But it is God who has called us here, and what is impossible becomes possible.[36]

White concluded her letter with gratitude for the unity that existed between her family and the students. The students were the most important people at FATEB, and she had seen them grow intellectually and spiritually throughout the year.

The leadership crisis that had swirled around the doyen a year earlier, in 1978, had been resolved sufficiently to enable FATEB to conduct its second year of classes successfully. But criticism of White from external sources had not ceased. Reflecting on those difficult early years, Zokoué said later, "Hocking continued to oppose White and FATEB from outside the institution. He had the ear of some of the American EFMA/IFMA mission leaders, and he persuaded the Grace Brethren pastors to cease supporting

---

34. Paul White, FATEB information Bulletin no. 5, May 1979.
35. Arline White, letter to friends, 6.1.79, in French.
36. Arline White, letter to friends, 6.1.79, in French.

FATEB. The bitterness of Hocking was evident throughout White's tenure as Doyen."[37]

1979-1980: EXPANSION OF FATEB'S CAMPUS

In 1979, the executive committee of AEAM met in Nairobi from July 2–4. This body was accountable only to the AEAM General Assembly. General Assembly decisions concerning FATEB took precedence over any decisions made by the AEAM Theological Commission. The fundamental question that persisted was whether White should remain as doyen of FATEB. AEAM's President Odunaike reported on his visit to Bangui 12 months earlier when he had spoken in depth with all the parties involved in the conflict. He observed that the doyen exercised a strong influence on the students regarding how the seminary was run. Odunaike didn't think this was entirely good for the students. He also observed that Hocking involved the local pastors in seminary affairs more than was necessary or desirable under the circumstances. The attempt of Isaac Zokoué, president of FATEB's board of governors, to obtain the votes necessary from FATEB's General Assembly to determine a specific course of action failed to receive a sufficiently large response, though of those who did vote, the larger number voted for White to be replaced. Rather than leave the question of White's leadership without a clear answer, the AEAM executive committee decided to act.[38] In this case, the executive committee sent a message directly to Isaac Zokoué instead of going through the Theological Commission.

The executive committee first expressed to Isaac Zokoué their disappointment that he had not exercised the initiative needed to resolve the problem. The executive committee then directed Zokoué to dismiss Dr. White, effective at the end of the 1978–1979 academic year. In addition, they asked that Zokoué inform White, and White's mission organization, as soon as possible of this decision, and that White leave the campus by August 31, 1979, at the very latest. The executive committee also warned the board of governors that failure to execute this decision would be viewed as an abandonment of its administrative responsibility and that the executive committee would be obligated to take further measures. The executive committee then concluded with expressions of appreciation to Zokoué and

---

37. Isaac Zokoué, "Founding of FATEB," 2–3.

38. AEAM, minutes of the executive committee, Nairobi, 7.2–4.79, 2–3, regarding the AEAM Theological Commission.

to White for all their work, sacrifices, and devotion in the management of FATEB.[39]

This action of the executive committee in July 1979 risked the closure of FATEB. Zokoué, president of FATEB's board of governors, reported receiving a letter from the executive committee of AEAM directing him to dismiss Paul White. Zokoué knew that this would result in the closure of the seminary. He responded to the executive committee that he would resign from the board of governors rather than close the school. President Odunaike, on behalf of the AEAM executive committee, then wrote directly to White, telling him to leave FATEB. White responded to Odunaike saying that he would leave FATEB only if Zokoué asked him to do so. In the end, Zokoué never did ask White to leave FATEB, but he did resign from the board of governors. Zokoué was replaced by Dr. Marini-Bodho of Zaire. As a result, despite the action of the AEAM executive committee and the intervention of AEAM President Odunaike, White remained as doyen of FATEB. By this time, the executive committee realized they had made an unwise decision in seeking White's dismissal and so took no further action.[40]

By January 1980, the third school year was well under way. Both Arline and Paul White wrote reports on the progress of their work. Arline White remarked that over 100 people were living on campus and that they spoke 10 different languages. Her objective was seeing that all members of a student family were being equipped for ministry, not just the thirty-two men and one woman in the degree program. The other student wives had attended primary school for an average of six years and generally had difficulty with the French language. Though they had been offered classes during the first two years, Mrs. White decided to organize the program more formally. Thus, in the 1979–1980 school year, the wives were expected to attend school for two hours each afternoon. One hour would be devoted to French and sewing and the other hour to Bible study and Christian service. To make this feasible, care was arranged for babies and young children during the time these women were in class. Occasionally, Mrs. White brought children into the women's classes, taught them a lesson while the "mamas,"

---

39. AEAM, minutes of the executive committee, Nairobi, 8.2–4.79, 3–4.

40. Isaac Zokoué, "Founding of FATEB," 2.

See also Dirindo Marini-Bodho, letter to Paul White, 10.8.79, asking that he assist Tiénou to assume the direction of FATEB. He signed the letter as president of the board of governors. But he added that if Tiénou didn't arrive in Bangui, he asked White not to leave the seminary but to open the school for the new academic year.

as they were called, observed, sent the children back to their campus childcare locations, and then discussed with the women her methods of teaching and the materials she had used. Later, the women themselves began giving Bible lessons to the children.[41]

For the women's Christian service, Mrs. White took them to visit churches. She had formed them into a woman's choir in which they sang using five different languages. The women sang, and Mrs. White brought devotional messages to the women's church groups. The "mamas" took notes on Mrs. White's talks, later discussed them in class, and took exams on them. This part of the course for the "mamas" Arline White called "preaching."[42]

Mrs. White, who had studied child development in university, was not satisfied with the campus children simply being in childcare. She believed they could be learning at the same time as their mothers were learning. So, in the two thatched-roof circular huts where the preschool children were being cared for, she instituted an hour of French and an hour of Bible knowledge teaching each day. The children's memorization of Bible verses in French helped both their French and their biblical understanding to grow.[43] This would enable the whole family to communicate effectively in African countries where the French language was becoming increasingly important in both church and national life.

Paul White began his January 1980 report to FATEB friends with the news that on the night of September 21, 1979, Emperor Bokassa of the Central African Nation had been overthrown, and the republic had been restored. Bokassa had crowned himself emperor two years earlier on December 4, 1977. His overthrow in 1979 occurred when White was in Europe, seeking funding for FATEB's building projects. Mrs. White, her children, and the rest of the FATEB community lived in considerable anxiety during the hours after the coup until calm and order were restored by the French military.

White went on to report that FATEB's third academic year had begun on October 15, 1979, less than a month after the overthrow of the government. While White and Luméya managed the teaching for the first semester of the third academic year, 1979–1980, several visiting professors joined them for the second semester in March through June 1980. The same 33

---

41. Arline White, report on the formation of all the family at FATEB, January 1980.

42. Arline White, report on the formation of all the family at FATEB, January 1980.

43. Arline White, report on the formation of all the family at FATEB, January 1980.

students from the previous year had returned to campus, but lack of living space prevented the school from accepting a new class of students for FATEB's third year. Rumors of the closing of FATEB were circulating in September and October 1980, which undoubtedly depressed the number of applications as well.[44] Intense fundraising efforts continued by Paul White in addition to his teaching and administrative responsibilities.

The library housed 7,000 volumes. By the time FATEB's building funds were exhausted, construction of the administrative and classroom building had proceeded upward to the second-story floor. Then, in late December 1979, an $80,000 grant from a German organization provided enough money to pay for the rest of the construction. Another grant from friends in Switzerland enabled FATEB to offer financial aid to students who were unable to pay their fees. The next priority was funding student housing so that a new class of students could be admitted for the fourth school year in October 1980. White concluded his report with a request for prayers for the new president of the board of governors, Dr. Marini-Bodho, and an expression of his joy that FATEB was in fact fulfilling the strategic purposes for which it had been founded.[45]

The third school year closed officially on June 16, 1980. White noted in his 1980 mid-year report that there were many moments when the future of FATEB was not at all certain. Yet, he rejoiced that, with the help of God, the school had emerged with a bright future ahead. White also wrote of another professor who had taught at FATEB during the first half of 1980 in addition to himself and Nzash Luméya: Dr. Josaphat Paluku of Zaire. These three professors composed the core faculty for the coming fourth academic year, 1980–1981. White mentioned the names of five visiting professors who had assisted in the school year just ended: Marini-Bodho from Zaire; Abel Ndjérarèou from Chad; W. Chabrerie from Strasbourg, France; Paul Wells from Aix-en-Provence, France; and Steve Miller, also from France. About 20 new students would be enrolled in 1980 from Rwanda, Burundi, and Cameroon, bringing the student total to about 55. Another $200,000 gift from friends in Germany enabled the completion of 18 student apartments for the new school year and the completion of the administration-classroom building.[46]

44. Paul White, FATEB information Bulletin no. 6, January 1980.

45. Paul White, FATEB information Bulletin no. 6, January 1980.

46. Paul White, FATEB information Bulletin no. 6, January 1980. The donor of the $200,000 and the previously mentioned $80,000 grant was Hilfe für Brüder in Stuttgart.

The political change in C.A.R. the previous September had positive implications for FATEB. David Dacko, Bokassa's predecessor, was restored to power again as the new president of the republic. Although a Catholic, Dacko was open to Evangelicals and was appreciative of the work of FATEB. Dacko gave FATEB a tax-exempt status for the purchase of construction materials and offered an interest-free loan of $300,000 to accelerate construction, thereby reducing the impact of growing inflation. More importantly, he granted an additional five acres of land contiguous with the southern border of FATEB's campus to facilitate construction of other seminary buildings. Years later, this land became a fully integrated part of FATEB's campus, bringing the total campus area of the seminary to twelve acres.[47]

1980–1981: ADDING PROFESSORS AND BUILDINGS

As anticipated, for FATEB's fourth year, 1980–1981, Paluku became a resident professor along with White and Luméya, and he brought his wife and four children to reside on campus. Luméya, who was married to Mpemba in July 1980, was also resident on campus with his wife. White continued as doyen, but his family had moved to Strasbourg, France, because of the health needs of his wife, Arline, and the educational needs of their daughters. As doyen, White was on campus to get the new school year started and to teach from October 6 to November 14 before going to Strasbourg. He planned to return to Bangui from January 28 to March 13 and once more for the month of June. The wives of Paluku and Luméya carried on the work of Arline White with the student wives while she was in Europe. White's secretary, Madame Annie, directed the learning activities of the preschool children. A French missionary, Jean-Claude Boix, came to Bangui to manage the school's administrative affairs during Doyen White's absences. Six visiting professors taught at FATEB that year, arriving from various countries in Africa, as well as from Switzerland, France, and the United States. The construction of two student apartment buildings of nine units each, along with work on the administration building, neared completion, though capital investments were still needed. White's four-year term as doyen, scheduled to end in June of 1981, left him uncertain about his future work with FATEB.[48]

47. Paul White, FATEB Information Bulletin, July 1980.
48. Paul White, letter to friends of the family and FATEB, January 1981.

CHAPTER 4

Early African Leaders—Josaphat Paluku, Isaac Zokoué

1981–1982: GRADUATING THE FIRST STUDENTS

FOLLOWING THE END OF FATEB classes on June 28, 1981, AEAM's Fourth General Assembly was held in Malawi in September. At that assembly, Dr. Josaphat Paluku was appointed doyen of FATEB, becoming the seminary's first African chief executive officer. Paluku had been serving on the FATEB faculty under White's leadership for the previous year and a half. With Paluku as doyen, White accepted the position of academic secretary of the faculty. Dr. Maurice Ndondoboni was appointed as a resident professor, to begin teaching in the 1981–1982 academic year. Professors Paluku, Ndondoboni, Luméya, and White would at this point constitute the core of the faculty. Five visiting professors had also been invited to teach during the 1981–1982 school year.[1]

In early October 1981, White made flight reservations from France to Bangui for himself, Arline, and the three youngest of their children. After spending the 1980–1981 school year in France, the family had decided to live on campus for the 1981–1982 school year where White could keep the family together, continue teaching, and work with the 14 students in their final year at FATEB as they wrote their master's theses. The student population was expected to reach 60 in the degree program. Arline White would be responsible for the training of nearly 40 student wives and more than 100 children. The children's needs included nursery care, preschool

---

1. Paul White, letter to friends of the family and FATEB, 10.4.81.

activities, and primary school education. In the children's work, she would be aided by her daughters Paula and Elizabeth.[2]

As the 1981–1982 school year began, Paluku and White divided the academic program into a three-year bachelor's cycle followed by two years at the master's level, leading to a five-year post–secondary school master's degree. The degree program included 53 students; 37 student wives enrolled in the Women's School, and the children's programs cared for the remaining members of the student families. In their final year, 14 students were working on their thesis of 90 to 120 pages. In March 1982, Doyen Paluku and Paul White left for a month of fundraising visits in the United States. Housing for professors and an enclosure for the entire campus were important priorities for which funding was needed.[3]

On June 27, 1982, FATEB held its first graduation ceremony for the 14 graduates who had earned master of theology degrees. After five years of hard work and times of uncertainty about the future of the seminary, these students were ready to graduate. The ceremony was held in a sumptuous commercial building in downtown Bangui in the presence of C.A.R.'s President Dacko. These 14 master's degrees were among the first awarded in the country. Christians from throughout the capital proudly joined in the celebration.[4]

During their five years of work at FATEB, these graduates had studied both theological and practical disciplines. They had taken courses in the biblical languages of Greek and Hebrew and studied Old and New Testament interpretation, theology, the history of the church, pastoral psychology, African studies, and Christian religious traditions. Student practicums had included leading worship in chapel, participating in evangelistic efforts, organizing youth camps, and teaching religion in the public high schools. In their final year, the students were involved in specialized church-related internships. Community life on campus was designed to nourish intelligent and practical piety. The campus community fostered a close association between students and professors as well as fellowship that centered on Jesus Christ and the Scriptures.[5]

From the founding of FATEB onward, a continual effort had been made to equip the entire family for Christian service in African cultures. In

---

2. Paul White, letter to friends of the family and FATEB, 10.4.81.
3. Paul White, letter to friends of the family and FATEB, 3.30.82.
4. Paul White, letter to friends of the family and FATEB, 11.7.82.
5. FATEB brochure, 1982.

addition to the training offered to the wives in family development, household management, and economic skills, the children were taught reading, elementary mathematics, French language, and Bible content.[6] FATEB faculty and administration had persevered for five full years to see the first class of students graduate.[7]

As a participant in the nearly five years of work between the decision to establish a francophone seminary in January 1973 and the beginning of classes at FATEB in October 1977, and having read the correspondence on which the above narrative is based, I would like to make several observations. First, the initiative of Nigerian Byang Kato as general secretary of AEAM and as head of its Theological Commission was essential to beginning the work that led to the founding of FATEB. Second, the negotiations of American Don Hocking with the Central African government were essential to the decision of C.A.R.'s President Bokassa to grant seven acres of choice land for the seminary project. Third, the work of Isaac Zokoué, a Central African, in representing the emerging association of evangelical churches to the C.A.R. government, in managing the interview with the chief of state, and in guiding the early days of the school as president of FATEB's board of governors and its General Assembly was essential to a successful launch of the seminary. Finally, the role of Paul White was critical in planning, communicating, and fundraising before the seminary program began and in administration and teaching during its first five years of operation. He was challenged by conflict over institutional values, management methodology, and struggles by various individuals for control. That FATEB exists today as a thriving educational institution 52 years after its conception would have been difficult to predict during the first decade that followed the AEAM meeting in Limuru, Kenya, in 1973.

1982–1983: LEADERSHIP TRANSITIONS

The state of FATEB as an institution during the new 1982–1983 school year was still fragile. The challenges it faced were daunting for its administrative leaders and its board of governors. Forty-seven students and their families were living on campus.[8] Sixteen new students had enrolled in 1982, coming from Zaire, Central African Republic, Chad, Angola, and Madagascar.

---

6. FATEB brochure, 1982.
7. Paul White, letter to friends, 11.7.82.
8. Josaphat Paluku, newsletter no. 11, March 1983.

About 80 children of the students could be numbered on campus that school year. The student body had come from eight different francophone countries and multiple ecclesiastical traditions. Construction of the three-story building for both administrative offices and classrooms was almost complete. Students were already meeting in two of its classrooms. The original one-story academic building was being remodeled to provide classrooms for the Women's School, a reading room for the women, and another room for the children. Four full-time professors composed the resident faculty. In addition, two missionaries living in the country served as visiting professors.[9]

The first fourteen FATEB students who completed five years of post-secondary school classes leading to a master's degree in 1982 were joined by nine more graduates in 1983. Of these twenty-three initial graduates, ten began serving as pastors, seven more taught in pastoral training schools, and four became university chaplains. Two graduates did not go into full-time Christian ministries: one of them taught in a secondary school, and the other enlisted in the national army.[10]

The 1982–1983 academic year brought Paul White's work in Bangui to a conclusion. Before coming to Bangui, he had been serving on the Island of Reunion but had attended the AEAM meeting in Limuru, Kenya, in February 1973 when the decision was made to create two graduate schools of theology in Africa. White recalled hearing an African who had stood up in a meeting in Nairobi a decade earlier and asked, "How long are we going to be obliged to go to Europe or America to become theologically well trained? Isn't it time to create theological seminaries on this continent?" This was the question that had triggered the chain of events that resulted in his becoming doyen and his family moving to Bangui in October 1977 to help found the Evangelical Theological School of Bangui (known soon after by its French acronym, FATEB). By 1983, White believed that this Evangelical seminary in francophone Africa was "solid and producing good fruit."[11]

July 5, 1983, was the final full day of Paul and Arline White's nearly six years of service together at FATEB since classes began in 1977. But in 1974, White had been made responsible to find financing for the project, to recruit professors, and to propose a program of studies. This was a full-time job for three years before classes began. White left with words of gratitude

9. Josaphat Paluku, letter to Van Barneveld, 3.21.84.
10. Josaphat Paluku, letter to Van Barneveld, 3.21.84, 2.
11. Paul White, letter to friends, 3.26.83.

to God for his faithfulness and for the courage and grace to complete the part of the seminary project for which he was responsible. He expressed his optimism for the future of FATEB and for the leadership team that followed him. He was confident that FATEB had been well established and was effectively carrying out its founding mission.[12]

1983–1984: GENEROUS HELP FROM FATEB FRIENDS

In 1983, as FATEB began its seventh school year, the library had grown to 8,000 volumes. An American librarian came to campus from the USA for six months that year. She set up a classification system and put the library in good order.

With the departure of the first doyen's wife, Arline White, the Women's School needed a director. The wife of one of the professors, Christine Ndondoboni, was able to assume direction of the school. To provide education for the preschool children of married students, Adé Mokoko, an African woman from Zaire (today the D.R. Congo) and a recent graduate of Moody Bible Institute, USA, came to FATEB and assumed that responsibility.

Finding housing for professors continued to be a problem, but a gift from the Evangelical Lutheran Church of Württemberg, Germany, gave funds for the purchase of a home near campus for a resident professor. Another German organization, Hilfe für Brüder, provided funds for building a security wall around the perimeter of the original seven-acre campus. An earlier grant from Hilfe für Brüder had helped to complete construction of the three-story administration-classroom building.[13]

Even with a larger faculty, Doyen Paluku needed to teach 15 hours a week. He had grown up in a rural area of northeastern Zaire, and he knew from personal experience that many local churches had pastors with little or no formal training. Paluku's central vision for FATEB was "Train teachers who will train others." The doyen was deeply concerned about the class of students to be admitted in the coming 1984–1985 school year. Student housing space was so limited that there would be room for only two new students. FATEB needed more student housing, and they urgently needed someone capable of managing the new campus construction that additional students would require. Requests for help were sent to Europe,

---

12. Paul White, letter to friends, 7.5.83.
13. Paul White, letter to friends, 7.5.83.

to North America, and to the mission agencies whose churches had sent students to FATEB.[14]

For the school to take advantage of visiting professors from Africa, Europe, and North America, the academic year was divided into eight segments of four weeks each. Professors coming to campus for only four weeks could teach one or two entire courses during these concentrated segments. The first opportunity to teach at FATEB accorded to me as a visiting professor came during a four-week period from March 16 to April 13, 1984. I taught a 30-hour theology course, the Doctrine of God and Creation, a 30-hour course in church history on the history of the Reformation, and a 20-hour seminar called the Role of the Church in Development. In addition, I consulted with the doyen on administrative and development issues at FATEB and spent time in counseling with students on matters related to their master's theses. This segmented school year facilitated the work of short-term visiting professors, though it somewhat complicated the schedules of the resident faculty.[15]

During that month on campus, I was impressed with the morale of the students. Most of them evidenced deep commitment to serve the churches in Africa. The friendships forged among students from various countries and different church backgrounds prepared them for future cooperation and broadened their vision for Christian ministry in Africa.[16]

Additional assistance came to FATEB from a small non-profit organization created in the United States in May 1984. Bruce Fleming, a missionary with the Evangelical Free Church of America, was responsible for incorporating this organization called Africa's BEST, Inc. (ABI). Its purpose was "to raise funds for the Bangui Evangelical School of Theology, Central African Republic, and to distribute funds to BEST (the English acronym for FATEB), or to projects and personnel affiliated with BEST," or to other similar organizations. Its mission was to assist BEST in "training pastors from Evangelical Churches in all of French-speaking Africa." A small group of men and women in Minneapolis, Minnesota, USA, worked with Bruce Fleming as volunteers to make ABI effective in carrying out its mission of helping support BEST. Fleming began sending newsletters and organizing

---

14. Josaphat Paluku, letter to FATEB friends, 12.30.83.
15. Jack Robinson, letter to friends, 4.1.84.
16. Jack Robinson, report on BEST, September 1984.

dinners to interest people in BEST, and the growing circle of such people were known as "BEST Friends."[17]

By this time, it was relatively easy to see several critical needs of FATEB that were challenging its leaders: (1) an applied learning program that would equip students for Christian ministry; (2) professors, staff, and learning resources necessary to carry out the learning program; (3) students ready to grow spiritually and intellectually and who wanted to serve God and Africa through church-related ministries; (4) campus facilities adequate for students and their families to live and learn in residence; (5) friends, churches, and foundations willing to pray, to work, or to contribute financially to help sustain FATEB students and the institution. The student financial needs were especially acute. Churches that sent students to FATEB were required to contribute financially to their training, but in general, their resources were meager. Thus, ABI proved to be a great encouragement and help to FATEB in the 1980s.[18]

Encouragement also came from some highly visible and greatly respected Evangelical leaders. FATEB had been created by the Association of Evangelicals of Africa and Madagascar (AEAM), a continent-wide association that was, in turn, a member of a global association, the World Evangelical Fellowship (today called the World Evangelical Alliance). The general director of the World Evangelical Fellowship in 1984 was David M. Howard, a well-known Evangelical leader. His public endorsement of FATEB was significant for the institution. He released the following statement on behalf of this global association:

> With the explosive growth of the church in Africa today and the rapid advances of modern civilization there, it is imperative that leaders of the church be trained in their own cultural context. BEST is providing graduate seminary-level Evangelical theological training in French speaking Africa. The World Evangelical Fellowship, in cooperation with our brethren in AEAM, is pleased to endorse BEST as the key training center for church leaders in francophone Africa today.[19]

The Rev. John Stott was another prominent Evangelical leader at that time. Doyen Paluku wrote in March of 1984: "FATEB is a strategic ministry. Rev. John Stott [of All Souls Church in London] visited us recently and

17. Jack Robinson, letter to friends, 4.1.84.
18. Africa's BEST, articles of incorporation, May 1984.
19. David M. Howard, report to AEAM General Council, 6.17–18.83.

was deeply impressed."[20] Later, Stott returned to Bangui to record a video interview in which he endorsed FATEB and the significance of its pastoral training ministry for preserving the biblical fidelity of African churches to the Christian faith. Considering the struggles of FATEB's administrators to help this seven-year-old educational institution survive, the support of world Evangelical leaders like Howard and Stott was tremendously encouraging.

In this 1983–1984 academic year, FATEB's students wanted their voices heard beyond the FATEB campus. In June of 1984, the students released an edition of their 22-page academic journal, *Phos*, the title meaning "light" in Greek. The mission of this periodical was to serve African theologians who wished to reflect on the word of God and its role in African life. They hoped it would be read throughout francophone Africa and western Europe, especially in seminaries and theological schools. The articles in *Phos* reflected the interest of the students in how the Scriptures informed African readers who were challenged by problems that differed from the issues addressed by theologians of the West. Students were particularly concerned to clarify their own identities as the beloved of God after decades of dehumanization and marginalization under colonialism. Concerns such as these could be discerned in the articles the students wrote for *Phos* in 1984.[21]

1984–1985: COMPLETION OF A THREE-STORY ACADEMIC BUILDING

In the late 1984, Doyen Paluku sent good news to friends and supporters of FATEB. The new three-story academic building would be essentially completed by Christmas. Administrative offices were planned for the ground floor, classrooms and library for the second floor, and more rooms for classes on the third floor. With the near completion of the new building, Doyen Paluku decided to convert two of the ground floor administrative office spaces into temporary sleeping quarters for eight unmarried male students. Additional space for three other students was created elsewhere on campus. Instead of having rooms for only two additional students, FATEB enrolled 13 new students in 1984, bringing the total degree program enrollment to 57 students. Ten French-speaking African countries were represented in the student body. Because the new academic building had received a fresh

---

20. David M. Howard, World Evangelical Fellowship statement on BEST, 5.10.84.
21. Josaphat Paluku, letter to Van Barneveld, 3.21.84.

coat of white paint, the eight students assigned to the sleep there facetiously announced that they were living in the White House![22]

Doyen Paluku had hoped that the Flemings would serve in Bangui during the 1983–1984 school year, but that did not happen.[23] However, at the beginning of the 1984–1985 academic year, the cadre of professors increased, and it included the Flemings. They arrived in Bangui as missionaries under the Evangelical Free Church. Joy Fleming was assigned to teach Old Testament and Bruce Fleming to teach Practical Theology and Missions. Thomas Touangai, a FATEB graduate of 1982 and a member of the Baptist Church in Bangui, also joined the faculty at that time to teach Greek, Evangelization, and the History of Revelation. Dr. Ndondoboni, from the Baptist Church in Zaire, taught Hebrew and Practical Theology. Göran Janzon, a Swedish Baptist missionary in the Central African Republic, came to teach Anthropology, Missions, and New Testament. Dr. Paluku, from the African Inland Church in Zaire, taught Theology. These six served as resident professors at FATEB for the 1984–1985 school year. Five visiting professors from Europe and one from the United States also taught courses during the year, along with a local FATEB graduate and six professors from the University of Bangui. That year, the seminary enjoyed a well-qualified and diverse faculty. As for bibliographic resources, Dr. Paluku expressed the desire to see the library's holdings increased to twenty thousand books in the following two years.[24]

Finances were urgently needed to complete construction of a block of 18 student-family apartments and for the day-to-day operations of the seminary. In addition, construction began in 1985 on a twenty-room dormitory building that could accommodate up to forty single students with two to a room. Called the "Celibatorium," from the French word for an unmarried person, *célibataire*, its completion didn't occur until well into the 1985–1986 academic year. In the meantime, several of the single men continued to live provisionally in administrative office spaces.[25]

Maintaining an adequate cash flow for operational expenses was difficult since the students were not able to pay for the real cost of their education. Their fees were $1,150 per year for unmarried students and $1,450

---

22. Josaphat Paluku, FATEB Information Bulletin no. 14, December 1984; Bruce Fleming, letter to Allen Lutz, 10.18.84.

23. Students of FATEB, *Phos* 4 (June 1984).

24. Students of FATEB, *Phos* 4 (June 1984).

25. Students of FATEB, *Phos* 6 (1986).

per year for married students. This fee structure included money for books, housing, a food allowance, and tuition. Later, student fees would be used only for tuition.[26]

From 1979 to 1983, FATEB had been assisted in campus maintenance and accounting by a European, Mr. Boix, who had come to live and work in Bangui with his family. But following their four years of service at FATEB, the Boix family had returned to France, and Doyen Paluku needed help in business and personnel management. No one was found for this position until, in March of 1985, an American, Herb Lea, arrived at FATEB with his wife Susan and their three children. The work Lea was given to do included bookkeeping, the paying of employees, supervising 20 workers, communicating with government officials, purchasing, and managing the campus bookstore. When he and his family arrived on campus, the entire student body came out to greet them with shouts and cheers.[27]

The Leas came to FATEB on loan from the Africa Inland Mission. In addition to Lea's work as business administrator and bookkeeper, Susan Lea, a nurse, became involved with the work of the campus clinic.[28] Health issues, in a city where medical help was limited, became a matter of life and death. In early 1985, a student wife at FATEB passed away from childbirth complications, and her newborn child survived only a few days. About the same time, the three-year-old son of faculty member Touangai sustained severe burns over 10 to 15 percent of his body, though he managed to survive. Malaria was also a constant threat, often hindering many students in their studies. In early 1985, Susan Lea contracted hepatitis. Then, in August 1985, an epidemic of diarrhea and vomiting among infants and small children hit the campus. Several children were hospitalized due to dehydration. The campus nurse was receiving two or three cases a day to care for. The outbreak was traced to an overflowing septic system, made worse by the unavailability of a city sewage disposal truck. Polluted puddles in the courtyard of the duplexes triggered the infections. Though several children were gravely ill, none died. Battling health problems was no small task for the FATEB staff.[29]

Later in 1985, the Flemings reported on their first year of teaching in Bangui. They wrote that the Central African professor Thomas Touangai,

---

26. Herb Lea, newsletter, 6.8.85; ABI, BEST News, October–December 1985.

27. Herb Lea, letter, 6.8.85; ABI, BEST News, October–December 1985.

28. ABI, BEST News, December 1983; Herb Lea, newsletter, April 1985.

29. ABI, BEST news release, May 1985; Herb Lea, newsletter, 6.8.85.

in addition to teaching Greek and Hebrew, had in 1985 become chairman of the translation team that was putting the Bible into the local language of Sango. He had been elected head of the Central African Association of Evangelicals and was serving as acting pastor of a large church in the city. The Flemings were impressed with the significant impact already being made by this graduate of the seminary.[30]

1985–1986: STRUGGLING OVER DIVERSE THEOLOGICAL VIEWS

As the 1985–1986 school year got under way, 13 French-speaking countries were represented in that year's student body. Many student applications were not accepted because the campus housing was filled with 57 students and their families. FATEB was conducting a five-year academic program leading to a master of theology degree. In addition, the seminary offered a three-year diploma program for student wives, elementary school classes for older children, and a preschool for children under six years old. The combined numbers of student and staff family members amounted to about 200 people on campus that year. The 20-room dormitory for single students was almost complete. Up to 40 students could live there, including some married couples without children. Friends in Sweden sent playground equipment to FATEB, a gift that delighted the youngsters. A new professor and his family from France joined the faculty that year also. The German mission that had helped financially, Hilfe für Brüder, was preparing to send a trained librarian to the seminary, Martina Bastian. Eleven graduates from the 1985 class were already engaged in ministry: one was conducting Theological Education by Extension, four were teaching in Bible schools and institutes, two were serving as university chaplains, one had begun doctoral work, and others were serving as pastors in their respective countries.[31]

The students' desire to make their views heard beyond the campus remained strong. In January 1986 they published another edition of their journal called *Phos*. In the publication, Mavinga Nzita indicated that the fifty-seven students enrolled in the five-year program were composed of fourteen single and forty-three married students. He wrote, "The diversity of races, nations, and ethnic groups requires a special grace for living harmoniously in the community." He added that, with students in a building

30. Bruce Fleming, letter to friends, 8.28.85.
31. Bruce Fleming, newsletter, September–October 1985.

for singles, along with the apartments for married students, FATEB could enroll up to 80 students in the degree program. Mavinga anticipated the completion of an enclosure around the seminary's new additional five acres of land that might become a playground for the children. He also reported that 12 students would be finishing their master's theses before graduating in 1986.[32]

Campus security was compromised because the lack of funds had hindered the construction of a wall all around the campus. Thievery by off-campus individuals created fear and loss for families and the school. In March 1986, the final stage of the security wall construction got under way. The base of the wall was of cement, and an iron fence was grounded in the cement and extended above it to complete the campus wall.

The work of the American organization Africa's BEST, Inc., created in May 1984, was successful in raising funds for FATEB. John Walkup was the director and only full-time staff member of ABI. He was tireless in donor communications from his home in Minnesota. Gradually, the financial response of individuals, churches, and foundations grew, meeting a critical need for general operating funds, for student scholarship assistance, and for various capital projects.[33]

Doyen Paluku's challenges were not limited to providing responsible leadership for FATEB. He also struggled over theological disagreements with individuals on the board of governors. The theological issues became acute in the first half of 1986, during Paluku's final six months as doyen. The difference of convictions between the board of governors and Paluku ultimately resulted in his leaving the seminary.[34] The first disagreement concerned FATEB's statement regarding the Scriptures. Unlike the statement of faith approved by both the World Evangelical Fellowship and the Association of Evangelicals in Africa, the word "inerrant" had been added to the FATEB statement of faith by the AEAM executive committee in 1976. The cooperation of the Grace Brethren Church in the new seminary project depended on the addition of the word "inerrant" to FATEB's doctrinal statement.[35]

Paluku contended that the use of this word "is not the expression of the faith of Africans responding to questions of faith in their particular

---

32. Bruce Fleming, newsletter, October–December 1985.
33. John Walkup, ABI, Friends in Touch, 1986.
34. Breman, *AEA*, 258–60.
35. Breman, *AEA*, 258.

concrete situations. It is the expression of the faith of others, responding to the questions that come from elsewhere." He went on to say that inerrancy does not guarantee true faithfulness to the word because it results in cutting short critical hermeneutical questions.[36]

The way FATEB's statement of faith referred to Satan also troubled Paluku. He felt that it gave too strong a status to the person of Satan and not enough to the reality of evil. Furthermore, he observed that Evangelicals were divided over the question of Satan. He saw the reference to Satan as another example of a confessional statement that addressed questions that were foreign to Africa and in this way sowed division and discord instead of unity and peace.[37]

Unable to obtain the degree of liberty he desired from the board of governors for professional research, Paluku concluded that, out of love for FATEB, it would be better for him to leave the seminary, avoiding a break-up of the institution and instead restoring peace to the FATEB community. Paluku's colleagues pled unsuccessfully with the AEAM general secretary that FATEB have the same statement of faith as AEAM so that Paluku could remain. But Paluku felt that staying at FATEB would make him subject to fundamentalist restrictions. He preferred to leave with his freedom and emigrated to France where he began serving as pastor of a Reformed Protestant church there.[38]

1986–1987: APPOINTMENT OF A NEW DOYEN

After the departure of FATEB's second doyen, Josaphat Paluku, in July 1986, Bruce Fleming was made acting doyen until the appointment of Dr. Isaac Zokoué in October. In addition to the arrival of Zokoué, a librarian, Martina Bastian, came to campus on a two-year assignment to put FATEB's library books in order and to better organize student usage of the library resources.[39]

36. Breman, *AEA*, 258.

37. Breman, *AEA*, 259.

38. Breman, *AEA*, 260. I was able to reach Paluku on a Zoom call in 2023 to speak with him for 45 minutes. This was the first connection we had had in 37 years. It enabled me to express appreciation to him for the outstanding contributions he had made to FATEB during his five years as doyen that overlapped with his six years as a professor. He and his family had made great sacrifices in the conduct of his ministry at FATEB for which he deserved profound thanks.

39. Bruce Fleming, letter to Jack Robinson, 10.7.86; Susan Lea, report, 1986.

Early Leaders—Josaphat Paluku, Isaac Zokoué

Isaac Zokoué began his service as doyen at the outset of the 1986–1987 academic year. He had provided strategic leadership for FATEB ever since its inception, and his wise direction was greatly needed at this time in FATEB's history.[40] No leader at FATEB has had a more formative impact on this institution than Isaac Zokoué, whose direct influence upon it lasted for 40 years.

Zokoué was born in 1944, son of a Baptist pastor. In 1974, he married Odette, a pastor's daughter, who gave birth to five children: Deborah, Dorcas, Jean-Marc, Jonathan, and Irène. After primary and secondary school in Africa, he enrolled in the French Evangelical seminary of Vaux-sur-Seine (Faculté Libre de Théologie Evangélique). After graduation with a master of theology degree, he served as regional secretary of the International Fellowship of Evangelical Students in French-speaking Africa. He also served on the Lausanne Committee for World Evangelization and the Pan African Christian Leadership Assembly planning committee. Zokoué received a doctor of theology degree in Montpelier, France, in 1983, and a second doctorate in 1996 from the University of Strasbourg, France.

Zokoué had led the audience with Central African President Bokassa in 1974 and obtained a grant of seven acres of land for the FATEB campus. He served on the action committee that oversaw the construction of FATEB's first buildings. He was named chairman of FATEB's board of governors for its first two years, 1977–1979, and he continued his role as a member of FATEB's General Assembly.[41]

Zokoué taught courses in systematic theology during his 14 years as doyen from 1986 to 2000. His doctoral thesis, completed in 1995, focused on the mystery of the divine and human natures of Christ the Savior from an African perspective. Zokoué contributed to his country as well as to the seminary. Because of his strong ethical character and prominence as a religious leader, the government asked him to lead the Preliminary Committee for the National Debate in 1997 that was meant to find a way to end the cycle of coups and civil war in the country.

After stepping down as doyen, on September 1, 2000, Zokoué began a new role with FATEB, leading a project to create a Center for Theological Research in Africa. This center was designed to be part of the ministry of the Theological Commission of the Association of Evangelicals in Africa (AEA). The center was to serve as a place for theological reflection and

---

40. Jack Robinson, ABI president's report, June 1987.
41. Isaac Zokoué, five-year plan, March 1987.

for the dissemination of the results of research done by theologians at an advanced level. Zokoué also led the project to create FATEB's doctoral program in 2005.

In April of 1987, FATEB's ten-year anniversary year, I made a second visit to FATEB, to teach there for three weeks. I noticed many campus changes from what I had observed in 1984. The student dormitory project had become a reality, and the academic building housed the library as well as faculty and administrative offices and six large classrooms. Other campus additions included a volleyball court and playground equipment for the children. In addition to encountering new students, I renewed friendships with faculty and students I had met three years earlier. The depth of dedication I sensed in some of the most gifted students was impressive. The joy their lives expressed as followers of Jesus was contagious.

After teaching biblical theology and history of the Protestant Reformation to the men and women in my classes, I left Bangui in mid-May 1987 with four distinct impressions. First, this seminary was already making a strategic contribution to the church and its outreach in French-speaking Africa. Second, though operating on very modest financial resources, FATEB was being managed efficiently, maximizing its personnel and facilities. Third, under the leadership of its new doyen, Isaac Zokoué, the school remained firmly committed to historic, orthodox Christian teaching. Fourth, for FATEB to have a viable future, it needed a broad, sustained financial participation from Christians, both within Africa and outside it. At this time, students were paying nearly 20 percent of the operating costs but benefited especially from financial assistance from Overseas Council in the USA, Hilfe für Brüder in Germany, and TEAR Fund in Great Britain. FATEB's credibility with financial supporters and prospective students was enhanced through formal endorsements by the Evangelical Foreign Missions Association (EFMA) and the World Evangelical Fellowship (WEF).[42]

While in Bangui, I asked one of the students from Zaire, "Why did you come to Bangui for your master's in theological studies? You could have gone to a theological school in your own country or in Cameroon." He replied, "Because, having seen graduates from other schools, our bishops were more impressed with what they saw of the graduates coming from FATEB. They judge a school by its fruit." "What do they want to see?" I asked. He replied, "Pastors who help their people understand the Scriptures, who are

---

42. Jack Robinson, ABI President's Report, June 1987.

not materialistic, and whose lives reflect the reality of the biblical truths that they teach and preach."[43]

One of the elements that was shaping the thinking and character of those who studied at FATEB was the diversity of its student body. Coming from as far as Guinea in the west, Madagascar in the east, also from former French, Belgian, and Portuguese colonies, and belonging to different tribes with their distinctive languages, histories, beliefs, and practices, these young adults of various backgrounds studied together. They came from different church traditions: Baptist, Mennonite, Presbyterian, Anglican, Methodist, Pentecostal, Apostolic, Reformed, and Brethren, founded by a variety of mission agencies. The diversity of the students was also reflected in the faculty composed of Africans, Europeans, and Americans. The result of the intermingling of these many differences created an international learning environment at FATEB and an opportunity for students to deepen their understanding and relationships with the diverse peoples of their churches, the continent, and the world.[44]

Despite the multitude of different influences that marked campus living, there were other factors that tended to unify the members of this learning community in the heart of Africa. The mission of this institution was to assist students to prepare for work that would strengthen the life and outreach of the church in modern Africa. For this reason, internships in local city churches were an important part of their applied learning. When graduates returned to their own countries, many acquired administrative roles in their denominations along with the normal ministries of a pastor. But students not only experienced a unity of purpose in their Christian service in Bangui. Faculty members also nurtured them in their commitment to the person, work, and message of Jesus Christ as revealed in the Scriptures. Growing out of their devotion to Jesus, students needed to formulate positions that would stand the test of philosophical agnosticism, science without God, and the religious pluralism that still confronted the church throughout Africa and continued to grow in the public universities.[45]

One more factor that characterized FATEB from the outset, and that contributed to student development, was the African environment in which student learning took place. The pressing issues in Africa during FATEB's first decade of existence overlapped only partially with key issues

43. Jack Robinson, ABI President's Report, June 1987.
44. Jack Robinson, ABI President's Report, June 1987.
45. Jack Robinson, ABI President's Report, June 1987.

in Europe and North America. Fetishism, polygamy, tribalism, and hierarchical church structures challenged African Christians. Even the plight of the poor could not be dealt with in the same way it was being addressed in the West. Political corruption also had distinctive shapes in African context. Freedom to critically examine the life and thought of contemporary African churches was always important for FATEB students. Many students wanted to show how the Scriptures could shed light on problems in the churches that needed to be corrected. Traditional cultural practices in the congregations sometimes clashed with what the younger generations saw as unnecessary or unbiblical. The master's theses of the students, written in their final year, were often designed to provide practical help for Christian leaders who were dealing with contemporary church concerns and the cultural issues that impacted their congregations.[46]

In 1987, ten years after its founding and five years after its first graduating class in 1982, about 70 graduates and their spouses had entered various ministries in Africa's French-speaking countries that together comprised nearly 150 million people.

In his first year as doyen, Dr. Zokoué summarized the progress on FATEB's campus building development. He wrote that on two-thirds of the original seven-acre campus there had been built three professors' homes, ten student duplexes for twenty families, two apartment buildings for eighteen couples, a twenty-room dormitory for single students, a one-level Women's School classroom building, and a three-story academic building housing an eight-thousand-volume library collection, as well as six offices for professors and administrative staff, and five classrooms. A security wall circled the entire seven acres. In addition to the physical campus and its structures, the five-year master of theology program was functioning to capacity with its dedicated resident teaching staff and qualified visiting professors.

Dr. Zokoué then elaborated a five-year plan for the continuing growth and development of the seminary, from 1987 to 1992. It included the areas of personnel, students, buildings, and equipment. Student recruitment and operational financial goals were listed. Breakdowns of the six curricular disciplines and their faculty needs were indicated. A map of the campus showed proposed sites for new buildings. Budgets were included for each of the next five years.[47]

---

46. Jack Robinson, ABI President's Report, June 1987.
47. Isaac Zokoué, five-year plan, March 1987.

One curious aspect of the five-year plan was Zokoué's mention that FATEB was running out of space and that he was asking the board to investigate the purchase of additional property. In a board report of Africa's BEST, Inc., in the USA, its secretary, John Walkup, said that Doyen Zokoué voiced concern to him "over the apparent withdrawal of five acres thought previously to have been given to the seminary for much-needed campus expansion." The doyen had no explanation for this, nor did John Walkup. In 1980, the Central African president, David Dacko, had granted five acres to FATEB, in addition to the original seven-acre government grant, for the purpose of expanding the campus. The doyen had attempted to plan the development of this additional parcel of land but discovered that, somehow, it no longer belonged to FATEB. The mystery of the disappearance of these five acres along the southern edge of FATEB's seven-acre grant was subsequently revealed and then formally restored to FATEB in 1991.[48] It had been discovered that when the government real estate records were examined, the name of FATEB had been almost completely erased from the official list of land title holders and replaced with the name of a government minister. This minister had secretly and illegally changed the ownership of the five acres granted to FATEB by President Dacko, divided the land into small plots, and then sold them to unsuspecting Africans. His corrupt act created an enormous problem for FATEB when this theft came to light. But in the end, after difficult negotiations and considerable expense, the land was eventually restored to FATEB to complete the twelve-acre campus as it exists today.

When Adé Mokoko arrived on campus in 1983 to continue the work that Mrs. Paul White had begun with the nursery care of babies and the teaching of older preschool children, she was well qualified for this work. After three years, Mokoko wrote a description of what she and her assistants were doing.

> We have a nursery for the babies aged three months to 18 months. Then, we have a kindergarten department for the children that comprises two levels: a first level with 20 children aged 18 months to four years; a second level with 25 children aged four to five years. Our goal at FATEB is to train the whole student's family for the Lord's ministry. All these children belong to FATEB students except a few who come from off campus. Our kindergarten

---

48. John Bennett, West Africa trip report, 4.29–5.7.94, 2.

program is the same as the one taught in the State schools except that we add biblical teaching in ours.

Mokoko went on to explain that the children memorized Scripture and sang many Bible songs. She added, "More and more people from off-campus are asking us to take their children because they appreciate our teaching and discipline."[49]

1987–1988: RENEWED VISION FOR FATEB

As Isaac Zokoué began his second year as doyen in 1987, FATEB had conducted ten years of university level classes. The initial five years had led to the first graduating class. Reporting to FATEB's friends and supporters in mid-1987, Zokoué wrote of how FATEB's development still amazed him:

> It's been a decade of sweat, tears, prayers and blessings. In 1977, FATEB began with three professors, a handful of buildings, and 17 students. Slowly, the teaching team was added to, more housing was built, and more students were admitted. In 1982, the first graduates left FATEB for service in French-speaking Africa.

The doyen went on to write that now he could count current and former students from 12 different African nations, ranging from Guinea to Madagascar and from Chad to Angola. By the time he was writing, five more classes of students had obtained their degrees and had left for the churches and denominations that had sent them to FATEB. Dr. Zokoué wrote that ten years earlier, less than half a dozen African leaders had been trained in Evangelical theology at the master's level in all 17 of the French-speaking nations of Africa combined. In 1987, during the seminary's tenth year, with over sixty graduates already in their ministries, fifty-seven more students were enrolled in the master of theology degree program, taught by six full-time resident professors and over a dozen visiting professors from three continents.

Zokoué concluded his report by writing, "We are keenly aware of the need for more trained leaders in our rapidly multiplying churches. We want to tackle an aggressive growth campaign to reach the masses of Africa with the Gospel." This was how FATEB's second African doyen described the seminary he had agreed to lead and the vision he embraced for the future

---

49. Adé Mokoko, BEST children's school report, 1987.

of FATEB and its role in French-speaking Africa. It was a vision of FATEB graduates sharing the gospel message with other Africans.[50]

Roughly 200 men, women, and children, living together on the same campus, constituted the FATEB community in 1987. Even though they came from different countries and a variety of ethnic backgrounds, languages, and Protestant denominations, links of relationship were formed that made what happened to one person the concern of everyone in the community. The example of one student wife illustrates this truth. During the 1986–1987 school year, Embeke Mosongo, the wife of a Zairean student, observed the growth of a tumor on her neck that created great anxiety for her and her husband, Mosongo. The tumor's proximity to her brain made it life-threatening. Local doctors thought it inoperable, the Mosongos didn't know what to do, and the whole campus community was distressed.

Through newsletters and personal communications, individuals and churches in the United States heard about Embeke's health crisis and decided to help. Funds were raised so that Embeke and her husband could travel to Rochester, Minnesota, for expert diagnostic work at the Mayo Clinic. Leaving their four children in Africa with her sister, and pregnant with a fifth child, Embeke, with her husband Mosongo, flew to Minnesota. People there received them, providing extra clothing and emotional care until she could be admitted to the clinic.

After extensive testing, a consultation of physicians at Mayo Clinic concluded that surgery would leave her seriously impaired physically, so they declined to do surgery. As a result, the Mosongos began their travel back to Bangui, and to their studies at FATEB. My wife, Theo, and I were at the airport to receive them in New York City as they waited for their trans-Atlantic flight to Africa. We thought Embeke was returning home to die. Yet, we did not sense in either Embeke or Mosongo fear or regret. They simply prayed that God's will be done and boarded their flight home. When they arrived in Bangui, Dr. Zokoué called students and staff for a special day of prayer for this couple.

Four months later, Embeke's baby was safely born. Many people had prayed that Embeke's life might be spared, and in fact, at some point, the tumor stopped growing. Today, it is 38 years later. Recently, we heard from Mosongo, who told us that Embeke still carries the tumor on her neck but is still living. As a couple, they are serving the church in the D.R. Congo. Embeke thanks God for her children and grandchildren and is filled with

---

50. ABI, BEST News, August–September 1987.

gratitude for God's kindness to her and her husband. No one imagined such an outcome in 1987.[51]

1988–1989: COPING WITH HIV/AIDS

By the end of Dr. Zokoué's second year as doyen, August 1988, personnel issues at FATEB required special attention. Because of changes in the structure of doctoral programs in France, Zokoué felt it necessary for him to prepare a second doctoral dissertation. The board of governors granted him a study leave for the academic year 1988–1989. In Zokoué's absence, a five-member administrative committee was appointed by the board to manage the administration of FATEB. It was chaired by Valentin Bétalé, who had served previously as a member of the board but had become FATEB's business manager. Four other members of the committee were appointed: board member Vermond Koubeli, Pastor Doko-Manga, president of AEEC, Pastor Paul Changé, president of the UFEB church association, and a new missionary accountant, Miss Anna Best.[52] Under the committee's year-long oversight, the school functioned successfully.

Nzash Luméya, a professor from Zaire, had taught at FATEB from 1979 to 1982. In 1982, Luméya and his wife left to study at Fuller Seminary in California where he earned a doctoral degree. Luméya returned to Bangui in 1988, and with the collaboration of Thomas Touangai, resident professor of New Testament, was put in charge of academic affairs. Bruce Fleming, who had served as academic dean and acting doyen, was released to go on furlough for the 1988–1989 academic year. His wife, Dr. Joy Fleming, a professor of Old Testament, accompanied him. In 1988, FATEB lost a German professor who had joined the faculty in 1983. His contract was not renewed for the 1988–1989 academic year because he held theological positions that were inconsistent with FATEB's doctrinal statement.[53]

The American organization Africa's BEST had functioned effectively in soliciting financial support for FATEB since its creation by Bruce Fleming four years earlier in 1984. In 1988, its tireless administrator, John W. Walkup, was 78 years old and ready to retire. This organization was planning to turn its work over to another American non-profit organization, Overseas Council for Theological Education. This transition concerned

---

51. John Walkup, ABI, Friends in Touch, October 1987.
52. ABI, BEST annual board meeting report, 8.15.88, 1–2.
53. ABI, BEST annual board meeting report, 8.15.88, 1–2.

EARLY LEADERS—JOSAPHAT PALUKU, ISAAC ZOKOUÉ

FATEB leaders because the seminary was a growing institution in need of external funding, and they were not sure how strong Overseas Council's commitment was to helping support FATEB. Nevertheless, the transfer to Overseas Council did take place in mid-1988.[54]

Under the leadership of John Walkup, Africa's BEST had raised several hundred thousand dollars for FATEB and its students since ABI's founding in 1984. Not only was this small organization of volunteers about to be dissolved, but also the important job of financial management at FATEB was threatened by the departure of Herb Lea, who had done FATEB's bookkeeping and had overseen its business management for the previous two years. In early 1988, Anna Best, an experienced American Conservative Baptist missionary with skills in bookkeeping and financial management, was on the verge of retirement from her work in Senegal. My wife, Theo, and I had worked with Anna Best in Senegal in the 1960s and knew her well. A few months earlier, we had asked her if she would consider filling the urgent need for accounting and financial counsel for Dr. Zokoué at FATEB. She wrote a long letter in French to Dr. Zokoué in April 1988, offering her services to FATEB.[55] Zokoué extended an invitation to Anna Best to join the administrative staff, and she arrived in Bangui just before the annual board meeting of August 15, 1988. There, she became a member of the committee of five to manage FATEB during Dr. Zokoué's study leave in France.

The three-year program for student wives who were not enrolled in the degree program created interest in several of the churches in Bangui. This situation raised the question of whether women from the city should be admitted into FATEB's Women's School. Although expanding the program in this way did not happen in 1988, some years later FATEB did open the Women's School to applicants from the Bangui churches and enjoyed positive results.[56]

One of the skills taught to master's degree students from the outset was how to do research and writing. To graduate from FATEB, a student needed to select a topic for his or her project, have it approved by the faculty, be assigned a thesis director, and complete the writing of a paper of about 100 pages that showed the content and sources of the research undertaken and

---

54. ABI, BEST annual board meeting report, 8.15.88, 2–3; John Walkup, letter to Jack Robinson, 4.18.88.

55. Anna Best, letter to Isaac Zokoué, 4.15.88.

56. ABI, BEST annual board meeting report, 8.15.88, 3.

the conclusions reached. The completed document was then submitted to three professors who formed a jury, gathered to discuss the thesis with the student, and then, if the thesis was satisfactorily written and defended, assigned a grade to the student's work.

Up to 1988, student thesis evaluations by an academic jury were public events. Later, when the doctoral defense became public, the master's jury was made private. During the time when the master's students defended their work publicly, friends of the candidate were invited to be present at such events. Listening to a thesis defense contributed to the students' understanding of responsible academic research. In 1988, Musa Opiyo, a man from the staff of FATEB's sister school, the Nairobi Evangelical Graduate School of Theology in Kenya, came to Bangui for a board meeting and served as its secretary. While on campus, he attended a thesis defense and left the following record:

> Witnessing a final year FATEB student defend his thesis publicly was an experience I shall never forget. Ngarndeye Bako from Chad was defending his thesis entitled, "The Task of the Shepherd and its application in the Evangelical Church in Chad." The jury consisted of Professor Bruce Fleming, Professor Thomas Touangai, and Rev. René Daidanso, AEAM Associate General Secretary. The Board of Governors walked into a jam-packed assembly hall. Various choirs took turns singing while the candidate sat pensive behind a table covered with white cloth, and on top of which lay a vase with flowers, a small stack of reference books, some water and orange squash in bottles.
>
> Immediately behind the candidate sat his wife and children. The front benches were occupied by the Chadian Christian community in Bangui who had come to witness the big day for one of their "sons."
>
> There was silence as the chairman of the jury called the session to order and announced the purpose of the gathering. After a few acknowledgements, the director of the thesis summarized its development, its content and purpose, before posing some questions to the candidate. The candidate responded confidently and then went on to face the second member of the jury, Professor Touangai. After the usual pleasantries, he began asking the candidate questions. His questions, which were related to the text, were more technical. He challenged the bibliography, questioned the candidate's failure to consult other African works, and commented on the candidate's style of writing as "preachy." He contended that the candidate had cited many authors but had failed to articulate

his personal opinions or affirm his own position. The candidate worked hard to defend his work and agreed to make corrections where needed.

The third member of the jury, Rev. René Daidanso, questioned the candidate the longest. He commented on various "forms" in thesis writing that had not been followed. He also asked questions of a more practical nature. They aimed at clarifying the purpose of the thesis and its relevance to the Chadian church today. The candidate did his best to answer.

The jury then retired to deliberate while choirs began their singing again. The atmosphere was charged with tension as everyone waited expectantly for the jury's verdict. The candidate and his family were still but obviously apprehensive. After ten minutes, the jury returned and delivered their verdict while everyone was standing. The thesis had been accepted with changes required on page 22. A grade of 14 over 20 had been awarded. There were ululations [loud, protracted, high pitched vocal sounds], laughter and celebration at this announcement. Celebrations did not cease until almost 1:00 am the next morning.[57]

FATEB professors were intent on equipping students with sound academic research and writing skills. But they were also concerned that students not lose sight of the needs of the churches that had sent them to study. This is why most of the theses written at FATEB were designed to assist the churches in practical ways. I was once asked what distinctive needs of the African churches I thought FATEB was trying to meet through their educational program. Here follows my reply in 1988:

> At a conference of Evangelical African leaders not long ago, three crucial challenges facing the Church in Africa were identified: Islam, poverty, and lack of adequate church leadership. FATEB is seeking to graduate men and women with a vision for the unreached peoples of Africa. It provides training in community development to address the economic need. Most of all, FATEB seeks to enable its students to present the truth of the Scriptures in a way that helps people see how God meets them at their point of need. It is also committed to their growth toward maturity in Christ and provides opportunities for their spouses to grow along with their mate.
>
> Professors are hampered daily by the lack of first-class Bible study literature in French. FATEB provides courses in theological

---

57. ABI, BEST annual board meeting report, 8.15.88, 8–9.

English to help students take advantage of the rich resources of biblical literature that exist in English. It is also encouraging students to help create solid Evangelical literature in French.[58]

In early 1989, I made my fourth teaching visit to Bangui in six years. Theo traveled with me to teach as she had done in 1988. At this time, the HIV/AIDS epidemic was on the rise and creating fear among the students at FATEB. AIDS was considered a death sentence for people who contracted the virus, and it continued to be deadly for another eight years. Encountering people with AIDS or with the disease in their family saddened us deeply. Among Bangui's population, at least 15 percent carried the virus, and in many families, both parents were dying, leaving their children behind as orphans. A local Christian doctor gave a seminar on AIDS to the seminary students while we were there. One student asked, "What hope is there for me if I have contracted AIDS?" The doctor replied poignantly, "God loves you, and nothing can separate you from his love." Some of the students were angry with those who were infected. Not understanding how the virus was transmitted, they felt threatened by people who had AIDS. As a result of the seminar, the students began to realize that the churches needed the courage to minister to victims of the virus with compassion and with a clear witness to the life that never ends in Jesus Christ.[59]

Nzash Luméya and his wife, Mpemba, had begun the 1988–1989 school year together in Bangui. But then, Mpemba became ill. By Christmas time, they returned to their families in the D.R. Congo. In the following January 1989, John Walkup, director of ABI, asked for prayer for her and her two children. Jack Graves of Overseas Council wrote that Mpemba was "very ill." What most people did not know was that she had contracted HIV from a blood transfusion and was suffering from the symptoms of AIDS. At that time, there was no curative or therapeutic help available.[60] Furthermore, there was little understanding of the nature of AIDS in the local African population. AIDS had become a taboo subject, and those recognized as AIDS victims were often isolated and treated like lepers. A woman in California knew Mpemba during Luméya's years at Fuller Seminary and became aware that Mpemba had contracted HIV. In a letter to a friend, she said:

---

58. Jack Robinson, "Interview with Dr. Jack Robinson," 9.22.88.

59. Jack Robinson, letter to friends, March 1989.

60. John Walkup, memo to the ABI board, 1.4.89; Jack Graves, Overseas Council letter to ABI related people, 1.10.89.

> I wrote to Mpemba asking her if she could bring herself to share [with others that she had AIDS]—despite the cultural taboos and the risks. What courage it would take. I have been weeping for her, finding the pain of her isolation, separation, emotional and physical condition unimaginable. I pray that God will protect the Luméyas and at the right time be able to open up [for them] the door of compassion and wisdom.[61]

At the end of January 1989, Luméya and the older daughter returned to Bangui so that he could carry out his teaching responsibilities. But Mpemba's health was such that she and their younger daughter stayed in the D.R. Congo with Mpemba's sister. Luméya flew to the D.R. Congo several times to visit his wife and was there with her on May 20, 1989, when she passed away. The FATEB community grieved her loss deeply. Following the local African tradition, an all-night service was held to comfort those grieving the loss of this beloved wife and mother. Over 200 people from the campus and Evangelical churches in the city attended the meeting. Three church choirs sang, speeches were given, and Luméya told of Mpemba's last days and her strong faith as she faced death. Pastors and Christian leaders assured Luméya and his children of their prayer support. The night was marked with hymns and prayers, and the memorial service ended at five o'clock the following morning. This event was planned to comfort Luméya, but as one FATEB staff member said, "We all needed that meeting."[62]

Isaac Zokoué spent the 1988–1989 school year on a study leave in France, but his departure reduced the capacity of the seminary to raise funds for general operations. Anna Best did all she could to manage the finances of FATEB as efficiently as possible during this very difficult school year. The seminary budget ran a deficit, and income failed to meet the operational expenses. By November 1989, FATEB's debt amounted to $23,500.[63] Anna Best wrote to many foundations seeking additional financial support but without much positive response.

Despite these challenges of the 1988–1989 academic year during the doyen's absence, FATEB remained stable under the guidance of the temporary administrative committee. Three people provided outstanding leadership. Valentin Bétalé had served for many years as a pastor and Bible institute director with the Evangelical Baptist Church coming from the

---

61. Kathy Naramore, letter to Jack Robinson, 3.1.89.
62. Anna Best, newsletter, July 1989.
63. Anna Best, newsletter, November 1989.

Swedish Baptist Mission in the Central African Republic. He was put in charge of student affairs, oversaw the work of all the campus employees, and managed the student internship program. His wife Anna, a woman of great practical wisdom and vitality, assumed the direction of the three-year program of the Women's School. Anna Best, veteran Conservative Baptist missionary in Senegal and Congo, handled the financial affairs and accounting for the seminary. The work of these three administrators contributed greatly to smooth operations and high student morale.[64]

1989-1990: UPDATING A FIVE-YEAR PLAN

As the 1989–1990 school year began, student enrollment remained strong. Fifteen of the seventeen French-speaking African countries were represented in the student body. Only Togo and Rwanda had not yet sent students. The first two students from Senegal enrolled in 1989. One from southern Senegal arrived with his wife and child. Another, a former Muslim, came from the church in Thies, Senegal, later becoming one of the country's outstanding Evangelical leaders.[65]

In late 1989, Dr. Zokoué updated the five-year plan he had created in 1987, focusing especially on the near future. For the first three years the plan included the appointment of a professor and the acquisition of a vehicle in 1990; the appointment of two professors and a secretary in 1991; the addition of two more professors and a second vehicle in 1992. For the library, the doyen's goal was two thousand new books and fifteen new periodicals each year for the next three years. In the area of construction, his aim was new buildings for the nursery, the infirmary, and four faculty apartments in 1990; a library building and a quadraplex for four more faculty in 1991; additional housing for faculty in 1992. In each year, equipment and materials would be needed for the work of the Women's School. For the infirmary, a refrigerator was needed; new medicines and vaccines were a necessity each year. Finally, annual additions of sports equipment, musical instruments, Bibles, and books for students figured into the plan.[66]

By January 1990, financial pressures had eased somewhat. Most of the financial obligations to the government had been paid off. Nzash Luméya was still teaching at FATEB. He did not contract the virus, and he and his

---

64. Jack Robinson, report on FATEB, 4.1.89.
65. Jack Robinson, report on FATEB, 4.1.89.
66. Isaac Zokoué, five-year plan, 2.

daughters were coping despite the loss of Luméya's wife, the girls' mother.[67] The biggest project in the minds of FATEB's leaders was the construction of a three-story building that would house the library, faculty offices, and a large meeting space. Projected cost was about $300,000. Overseas Council in March of 1990 proposed that they and Hilfe für Brüder accept responsibility for raising $150,000 each. This building would be a great asset to the campus academic and spiritual programs.

1990–1991: FACULTY CHANGES AND ECONOMIC ASSISTANCE

Despite an attractive five-year plan and substantial interest by donors in financing building projects, the struggle to obtain adequate operation funds remained. This problem became critical in 1991. At the same time, maintaining the theological orthodoxy of the faculty was also difficult. Although a professor from Germany had been released in 1988 because of his liberal views on Old Testament criticism, a bright student who had sat under his teaching had adopted his views. After graduating from FATEB, this graduate began teaching at the seminary. In January 1991, a FATEB board member from Senegal, missionary Don Penney, wrote to the board chairman, René Daidanso, expressing his concern about the theological beliefs that this young professor had supported in his master's thesis.[68] Discussions took place between Zokoué and the professor, and by the time of the board meeting in late January, the professor had decided to resign his position on the teaching staff and left FATEB on July 31, 1991.[69]

The economic state of FATEB worsened in 1991. Financial support from Overseas Council declined, and both student scholarships and faculty salaries suffered. Debts to the city for electricity and water grew. An agent came to campus to turn off the electricity in July 1991, but he was dissuaded by a partial payment made on the spot. Later, the campus water supply was turned off for non-payment of bills. Women on campus were obliged to walk to a nearby city school to draw water and carry it back to campus in buckets on their heads in typical African fashion. In the midst of this situation, an anonymous Central African intervened to pay off the roughly $5,000 owed to the government to restore campus water.

67. Anna Best, newsletter, 1.16.90.
68. Don Penney, letter to René Daidanso, 1.7.91.
69. Anna Best, letter to Jack Robinson, 2.20.91.

Board member Don Penney, with whom the financial manager Anna Best had worked for many years in Senegal, died in early 1991. This was a great sorrow for her. When funds for a Don Penney memorial were sent to FATEB, Anna discussed the use of the money with his family. In the end, they decided to use the funds to assist the seminary with its pressing needs for operational support.

The political situation in the country also deteriorated in 1991. The post office was on strike for weeks at a time. To exchange messages with key people and organizations in the United States, mail was often hand-carried by travelers returning to Europe or North America. Sometimes messages were sent back and forth by fax and occasionally by expensive long distance telephone calls. At times, angry local citizens declared Bangui a "dead city" (*ville morte*), which meant that appearing on the streets made one vulnerable to attack. Tear gas was used to break up mobs, and gunfire was occasionally heard. The Baptist Mid-Missions station outside of Bangui was attacked, looted, and burned in July 1991. The missionaries escaped with their lives, but it was never possible for them to return to their mission station that had functioned there for many years. Instead, they rented facilities in Bangui.

One bright spot in the 1990–1991 school year was the appointment of three resident professors at FATEB. Two of the new professors were Americans: Dr. Judy Hill and Dr. Rich Starcher. The third professor, Dr. Mfuta, arrived from Zaire. Starcher remained on the faculty only two and a half years, 1990 to 1992, deciding to leave in December 1992 to teach in Nairobi, Kenya. Dr. Hill came to Bangui in 1991 with Africa experience in both Ethiopia and Nigeria. Serving as professor of New Testament, she began the longest tenure of any FATEB professor in FATEB's history. After more than 20 years in residence on the Bangui campus, she has been teaching remotely for the past decade from the United States and continued her work with doctoral students in the seminary via the internet until October of 2024.

1991–1992: SIGNS OF FATEB'S GROWING IMPACT IN FRANCOPHONE AFRICA

Despite the political and financial pressures during the 1990–1991 academic year, the seminary managed to carry on. New classes began in 1991 with six resident and several visiting professors. Complaints by students earlier in the year were no longer heard, as all their courses were being taught. Even though mission leaders in the West had been warned that FATEB might collapse because of the lack of adequate financial support, the Africans were determined to carry on, no matter how difficult the situation became. After all, this educational project was not one created by people outside of Africa. It was founded by African Christians who wanted university level training for church leaders to take place in the African context. Western investment in FATEB was far less deep than that of Africans themselves. Africans had no guarantee that Christians outside of Africa would rescue FATEB if it were unable to continue operating. But when a student was asked what he would do if the school had to close, he replied, "I would just wait here until it reopened again."

Enrollment for the 1991–1992 school year reached 48 students in the degree program. They came from a wide range of church denominations and mission organizations, including the following: SIM International, Evangelical Free churches, Sudan United Mission, British UFM, Christian and Missionary Alliance, Lutheran, Grace Brethren, Baptist, Evangelical Covenant, Gospel Missionary Union, Anglican, Pentecostal, Mennonite, and WEC International.[70]

In 1992, Dr. Judy Hill sent a newsletter to her friends and supporting churches in which she wrote,

> The first week of July marked the end of the 1991–1992 school year at the Bangui Evangelical School of Theology. The flurry of final exams and the pile of term papers are now history, and another academic session has been successfully completed. Besides the six resident professors, nineteen visiting professors have helped us, some of whom have taught several courses. We thank the Lord that we were able to complete our entire academic program despite the various challenges along the way.
>
> This year's graduating class has ten members, eight men and two women. Each of these students, now at the end of their fifth year of studies, had defended a master's thesis before a panel of professors. In addition to the two wives in the master's program, the wives of six graduating men had completed the three-year Women's School program. Now we can send out eight couples, with their children, to the ministries for which they have been prepared. Eight couples might seem like the proverbial "drop in the bucket" compared to the needs in Africa, except for the fact

---

70. Isaac Zokoué, summary of the state of FATEB, 1992, 1–5.

that each of these couples is equipped to train many others for active participation in the ministry.[71]

By 1992, Dr. Zokoué had served for six years as doyen of FATEB, and the seminary had been training men and women for ministry for fifteen years since it begin classes in 1977. Zokoué provided a summary of what the school had accomplished:

> 119 students have graduated from the master's degree program, while 118 have been trained in FATEB's Women's School program. FATEB's graduates are involved in such ministries as theological education, Christian education, leadership of church associations, Bible translation, pastoral ministry, relief and development projects and para-church ministries. Several of the graduates are currently pursuing doctoral studies in Europe and America so as to be able to return to Africa as theological teachers.[72]

The master of theology degree offered six possible areas of concentration: New Testament, Old Testament, systematic theology, ethics, church history, and practical theology, including missiology. The three-year required program for student wives who were not enrolled in the master's program provided training in biblical studies and domestic sciences as well as primary health care and family development. "African churches need strong families where a wife can have as broad an influence as her 'degreed' husband," wrote Dr. Zokoué. FATEB was conducting a holistic program of leadership formation.[73]

In Zokoué's 1992 report on FATEB's progress, he referred to the campus primary school that was educating children of the students. Government schools had been plagued by strikes and occasional failure to pay teachers that prevented children from moving smoothly from one grade to another. Parents living at FATEB with their families responded by hiring teachers to come on campus to teach their children, thus creating a small primary school. Soon after, parents of children from city families asked if they could send their youngsters to the campus primary school. As the numbers of children increased, the FATEB administration decided to assume responsibility for managing the growing primary school. No one imagined at that time that these decisions would lead to the continued

---

71. Judy Hill, newsletter, 1992.
72. Isaac Zokoué, summary of the state of FATEB, 1992, 1–5.
73. Isaac Zokoué, summary of the state of FATEB, 1992, 1–5.

expansion of general education instruction to include a middle school and eventually a campus high school.[74]

By 1992, FATEB had six resident professors: two from Central African Republic, two from Zaire, and two from the United States. Visiting professors from the local university taught non-theological subjects such as philosophy, African literature, and English. Nine other visiting professors, from Africa, various nations in Europe, and the United States, had taught courses over the 1991–1992 academic year. On the administrative staff were the doyen, a campus manager, an accountant, the assistant academic dean, and a librarian. They were assisted by a typist, an assistant accountant, and a driver, plus five workers for campus maintenance. The Women's School was led by its own headmistress and an associate.[75]

By 1992, the library held over 10,000 volumes. Total student costs amounted to $8,000 a year, with $3,900 being tuition expense and $4,100 required for housing and living expenses. The cost of a ThM degree in the USA or France would have been many times as much. Furthermore, these studies took place in an African context where the graduates would be serving. Most students who studied at FATEB remained in Africa after graduation, so there was little "brain drain."[76]

1992–1993: BETRAYAL WITHIN THE CAMPUS COMMUNITY

During the 1992–1993 academic year, the basic financial situation of FATEB did not improve. At the same time, although the government shut down utilities for the campus more than once, unexpected gifts arrived during the year that enabled the school to continue. The faculty and staff saw this unplanned financial assistance as a gracious answer from God to their prayers.

The most disheartening event of the 1992–1993 school year was the attempt of a resident professor from Zaire, Dr. Mfuta, to force out Dr. Zokoué as doyen of FATEB and get himself installed as the new doyen. He sent a letter to several dozen mission agencies and financial donors of FATEB in Europe and North America. In his letter, he made many untruthful claims about Dr. Zokoué and accused him of corrupt management. But instead of writing this letter over his own name, he signed it in the name of the highly

---

74. Isaac Zokoué, summary of the state of FATEB, 1992, 1–5.
75. Isaac Zokoué, summary of the state of FATEB, 1992, 1–5.
76. Isaac Zokoué, summary of the state of FATEB, 1992, 1–5.

respected president of the student council, Maurice Sogoba. The professor then took the bundle of letters to the Bangui airport and asked an American visitor departing for the United States to mail them when he arrived home. The envelopes had no return addresses on them, but the man who received the letters posted them in North America as the professor had requested, adding his own return address.

Eventually, the author of these defamatory letters was identified, though the professor denied involvement even when confronted with compelling evidence. Dr. Zokoué was deeply discouraged by this betrayal, but he had to write letters to FATEB's international friends and supporters to explain what had happened. The student body president was angry that his name had been used in this unscrupulous way. As a result, his fellow students began boycotting the culpable professor's classes. Having no more students to teach, the professor was compelled to leave at the end of the 1992–1993 school year.

Anna Best had come to Bangui in 1988, during her early retirement years, to manage the financial affairs of the school and to serve as its accountant. In 1993, almost five years later as she approached her seventieth birthday, Anna Best felt that she needed to truly retire. A candidate to take over her responsibilities was identified, but at the last minute he decided he could not assume this financial work. Anna Best completed her service and returned to the United States. Pastor Valentin Bétalé, campus administrator and chaplain, and his wife Anna, headmistress of the Women's School, also left FATEB to respond to the call of their church in the western part of C.A.R. These open positions were filled by Pastor Bara Issa and his wife, Rebecca, from Niger. These two people had spent five years in school at FATEB and were both graduates of the master's program. They were well equipped for these new responsibilities.[77]

1993–1994: CRITICAL NEED FOR STUDENT SCHOLARSHIP FUNDS

In mid-1993, Theo and I were completing six years of teaching at a seminary on the east coast of the United States. By then, our children had finished their university studies and were living on their own. Our work at the American seminary was rewarding, while the challenges facing the seminary in Bangui were troubling. Making annual teaching visits to Africa

---

77. Isaac Zokoué, newsletter, December 1993.

while working full-time in seminary administration and teaching in the USA was becoming increasingly difficult for us. As we thought and prayed about what to do, we felt that it would be easier for the seminary in the United States to replace us on its faculty than it would be for FATEB to find personnel who had the experience and qualifications that would enable them to help the seminary there. So, after consulting with Dr. Zokoué and the mission society leaders under whom we had served in the 1960s and 1970s, we began to make plans to rejoin WorldVenture (formerly CBFMS) and to return to Africa residentially in 1994. Theo and I believed that this was the next right step for us to carry out our sense of calling to help train leaders for Christ's church wherever it seemed our experience and abilities would best fit. Our conviction was that francophone Africa was where we could serve most effectively.[78]

We had two main objectives in going to Bangui. First, to teach eight or nine months of the year. I would teach theology, church history, and missions, and Theo would teach English to French-language speaking students. All FATEB students had previously had their education in French, but as Evangelical scholars, they needed access to the rich Christian literature that existed in English. Theo could help them work with English language sources.[79]

In November of 1993 Dr. Zokoué wrote to me of the two main financial priorities for FATEB as he saw them: current operations and capital projects. The first included the cost of salaries, utilities, maintenance of buildings and equipment, and other running expenses. In this category, student fees covered only about a third of operating expense. Outside assistance was needed for the other two-thirds of the annual budget. To acquire such funds, FATEB needed additional partners from Europe and North America. For other projects, additional teaching and administrative personnel were needed, and funds for buildings and campus infrastructure as well. In light of this situation, Theo and I felt our two priorities should be, first, to teach in our respective disciplines until qualified African personnel could replace us, and second, to work with foundations, individuals, and churches that possessed financial resources until a sustainable financial base of operational funding could be established.[80]

---

78. Jack Robinson, letter to Jim Plueddemann, 7.31.93; Jack Robinson, future ministry proposal, 7.31.93.

79. Jack Robinson, newsletter, Fall 1993.

80. Jack Robinson, project proposal for FATEB, 11.1.93, 3; Isaac Zokoué, letter to Jack Robinson, 12.2.93.

Dr. John Bennett of Overseas Council arrived in Bangui on April 29, 1994, to visit FATEB and analyze its needs. Based on his report, Overseas Council would make decisions on financial grants for FATEB. One of Dr. Zokoué's major concerns was to continue the development of campus building projects. First, FATEB needed a library and multipurpose building. Second, the five-acre land parcel that had been restored by the government to FATEB on the southern border of the current property needed a surrounding security wall. At that time, the additional property did not have a protective enclosure, and people who had been sold plots illegally were living on it. Furthermore, when the government had renewed FATEB's title to this property in 1991, they had given the seminary a deadline of four years for development of the property, or it would be repossessed by the state. Faculty housing had been planned for part of the new property, and the people living there needed to be relocated before construction could begin. By 1994, FATEB had only one remaining year left to demonstrate its development progress, and a great deal of work and expense lay before FATEB's leaders.

The 1993–1994 academic year witnessed the loss of several professors. In addition to the departure of faculty member Mfuta, Paul Mpindi, a FATEB graduate from the D.R. Congo who had been teaching Old Testament, left for Calvin Seminary in the United States to pursue doctoral studies. Dr. Rich Starcher had left in the previous school year for Nairobi but was planning to come back to teach one course each semester as a visiting professor. Other visiting professors planning to teach did not always appear. The schedule of courses being taught lacked smooth sequencing. A Central African professor, Thomas Touangai, had so many responsibilities outside the seminary that he did not consistently complete his teaching assignments. Dr. Zokoué and Dr. Hill were both greatly appreciated by the students and provided consistently high academic standards and teaching for the student body. Dr. André Kouadio from Côte d'Ivoire and professors from the Netherlands were especially appreciated by the students.

In 1993, a second Evangelical seminary at the university level in francophone Africa was founded by the Christian and Missionary Alliance in Abidjan, Côte d'Ivoire, under the direction of Dr. Tite Tiénou. In May of 1994 just after his visit to FATEB, Dr. Steve Hardy of Overseas Council traveled to this new institution, la Faculté de Théologie Évangélique de l'Alliance Chrétienne, known under the acronym of FATEAC. Though some observers thought that the two schools might be competitive, Dr. Hardy observed a spirit of cooperation between them. The schools were not only a long distance apart but were located in different cultural and religious contexts. Muslim-Christian tensions were much more visible in Abidjan than in the Christianized areas of Central Africa where FATEB was situated.

Enrollment at FATEB was limited by the on-campus housing that could accommodate about 50 students. However, the most critical factor that Dr. Hardy observed was the lack of student scholarship support. Student applications each year were many times more numerous than the number of students to whom FATEB was able to award scholarships. In 1994, 71 applications were received but only 10 could find the financing needed to enroll. An increase in scholarship support in the following years resulted in a dramatic increase in the numbers of students able to come to the campus to study. Distinctive elements that attracted students to FATEB were its Evangelical character, its five-year academic program that combined both bachelor and master level studies, and its service to all 17 of Africa's francophone countries with their many Evangelical denominations. Students spoke often of the rich opportunity to study and interact with Christians from other denominational, ethnic, and national backgrounds. This diversity contributed to Evangelical unity in both central and western Africa.

By mid-1994, FATEB had graduated 140 students with the master of theology degree, and well over 125 women had earned diplomas from the Women's School. Dr. Zokoué reported that many former students, both men and women, who were engaged in ministries in francophone Africa, had written to express their appreciation for what they had received at FATEB. This fact encouraged him to believe in a good future for the school. Nevertheless, financial issues continued to challenge the seminary. A devaluation of the currency earlier in the year forced a reduction in the number of workers at FATEB.[81]

1994-1995: PRACTICAL VALUE OF VISITING PROFESSORS

The 1994–1995 school year was a year of transition for Dr. Zokoué and for FATEB. In 1983, he had earned a doctorate (DEA) from Montpellier in France. Before the academic reform of 1984, France had two levels of doctoral degrees. After that date, the educational institutions offered only

81. Isaac Zokoué, report on the 1993–1994 year.

a single degree for the research doctorate (PhD), considered to be a higher degree than the one Dr. Zokoué had earned in Montpellier. Since FATEB was planning to offer its own doctoral program, Zokoué and the governing board of FATEB believed he needed the university doctorate of France's new regime. He had enrolled in the University of Strasbourg after the reform of 1984, but ten years later in 1994 the University of Strasbourg informed him that he would have to complete his work in the 1994–1995 academic year or else abandon his doctoral project.[82] This meant that most of that school year he would be in France, and an interim doyen of FATEB would need to be found. Zokoué's budget of $15,000 for tuition and living expenses would also need to be funded.

By the time that Theo and I arrived in Bangui on December 1, 1994, to begin our residency in C.A.R., most of the needed financing for Zokoué's final year in Strasbourg had been acquired. He told us that he would be leaving for Strasbourg by the end of that month. When I asked him who would serve in his place during his absence he replied, "You will." Earlier that year I had written to him, saying that I would be glad to help as needed but that I would not serve as the interim doyen. I had also sent a message to the FATEB board chairman, René Daidanso of Chad, suggesting that he assume that responsibility. But Zokoué insisted that there was no other viable choice, even though Theo and I had already accepted a full teaching load for the remainder of the school year. So, that is how our transition developed. We survived the academic and administrative overload, and Zokoué completed his doctoral program by July of 1995.

Regarding campus development, much had been accomplished since classes had begun 17 years earlier. The campus was now composed of two buildings for married student families, one for single students, three staff residences, ten duplexes for twenty married students, a three-story academic building, a building for the Women's School, a children's school, an infirmary, an equipped children's playground, and an African kitchen. Still needed were a library, a multipurpose building, more staff residences, and an enclosure around the new five acres.[83]

In 1994, FATEB was beginning its eighteenth year of training, and Isaac Zokoué was commencing his ninth year as doyen. Several issues needed to be explored and decisions made: clarifying relationships with other francophone schools preparing people for ministry; setting priorities

82. University of Strasbourg, letter to Isaac Zokoué, 6.9.94.
83. Jack Robinson, letter to John Bennett, 6.10.94.

and elaborating plans for campus development; resolving the persistent problem of finding financial aid for students; minimizing the costs of training students; meeting the personnel needs for faculty and administrators; and building on FATEB's distinctive educational contributions that would best help the churches to which students would return.

FATEB had been criticized for its limited number of resident faculty. From the outset, visiting and local part-time professors had proved essential to meet the needs for teaching personnel. By 1994, there were 11 visiting professors who had been as consistent as residential professors in teaching courses in their various specialties. Furthermore, most of the men and women teaching part-time at FATEB were engaged in active ministry in Africa and beyond. They were modeling the kind of commitment to the church, its growth, and outreach that contributed to practical student preparation for ministry. They helped keep students in touch with the real world that was challenging the church in Africa. Regular visiting teachers included professors from Chad, Côte d'Ivoire, Zaire, Central African Republic, Kenya, Sweden, and the USA. However, the resident faculty was limited to five professors: Isaac Zokoué, who was absent much of the year, and Thomas Touangai, who was deeply involved with the Bible Society. The other resident professors in 1994–1995 were Dr. Judy Hill, Theo, and me.[84]

Two tragedies saddened the campus community. First, Chairman of the Board of Governors René Daidanso and his wife, Martine, lost their 19-year-old daughter, Kodoba, in a drowning accident.[85] FATEB's chaplain and campus administrator, Bara Issa, accompanied by the doyen's wife, Odette Zokoué, traveled to N'Djamena, Chad, to offer condolences to the Daidanso family on behalf of FATEB and the doyen.[86]

The campus community mourned a second tragedy, which occurred on August 31. Faculty member Thomas Touangai and his wife Marie-José lost their five-year-old little girl, Danielle, following a persistent illness. Because the family lived on campus, the FATEB community felt the death of this girl acutely. As hard as it was for the Touangais to accept this loss, the couple still went on to raise their five other children and continued their ministries of serving God and his people.

---

84. Jack Robinson, notes on conversations with Isaac Zokoué, 6.6, 9.6, 12.6.94; Jack Robinson, letter to Manfred Kohl, 3.12.94.

85. Tokunboh Adeyemo, fax, 1.10.95.

86. Jack Robinson, letter to René Daidanso, 1.12.95.

The lack of operating funds created financial pressures for the school, its faculty, and employees. Generous gifts from German Hilfe für Brüder, Swedish Örebro Mission, and Dutch Reformed Church sources were of tremendous help to the financial stability of FATEB in 1995. TEAR Fund in England had been providing generous scholarship help for students on a regular basis as well.

In the month of May 1995, detailed plans were made for fundraising efforts to be undertaken during the following months. A group of eight people met for four days, May 4–9, to formulate plans to strengthen FATEB in the years ahead. Dr. Manfred Kohl of Overseas Council facilitated these talks. Discussions were conducted on increasing student enrollment, an executive committee of the board of governors was established that would meet quarterly to make more timely decisions, and five leadership positions were clearly described to improve the school's management. Plans were made to upgrade the financial accounting system of FATEB, and several policy decisions were made affecting various areas of the administrative, academic, and social activities. A new scholarship policy was created to provide more help for students. Development of the campus buildings and roads were planned, and efforts were initiated to get the title and legal possession of the adjacent five acres of land that had been granted to FATEB years earlier. Cost estimates were made for additional buildings to house faculty, staff, and students. Plans were also made for a multipurpose building for the library as well as chapel services, lectures, conferences, social activities, and faculty offices. Clarifying these needs for FATEB's development provided a solid basis for the fundraising activities that were critical to the future health of the institution.[87]

1995–1996: MILITARY INSURRECTION AND EVACUATION OF FATEB PERSONNEL

At this time in 1995, Nupanga Weanzana, a member of FATEB's 1990 graduating class, indicated his desire to serve at FATEB, in both teaching and administration.[88] After in-person discussions, Nupanga was appointed vice-doyen at the beginning of the 1995 school year. Nupanga also expressed his intention to pursue doctoral studies in Old Testament after

---

87. Manfred Kohl, report on FATEB, May 1995.
88. Nupanga Weanzana, letter to Isaac Zokoué, 4.4.95.

some years of administrative work and then to return to FATEB to rejoin the faculty.[89]

Paul and Phyllis Schmidt agreed to transfer from their work in Zaire with the Evangelical Free Church Mission to manage the accounting and business affairs of FATEB in January 1996.[90] This was an administrative position for which competent direction was greatly needed, and Schmidt possessed the required professional training.

As this institutional activity continued, students were learning, doing research and writing, and graduating with completed master's theses. In June of 1995, a FATEB student committee published a 24-page edition of their magazine, *Phos*. Along with articles reflecting their concerns for the African churches and diverse pieces of information about FATEB, they listed the titles of the master's theses defended at the end of the previous school year: celibacy in the African context, the implications of Paul's discourse in Acts 20 for pastoral work, responsibility for creation care, church growth in the Baptist churches of Central African Republic, the role of the church in politics, the person of Christ in Muslim evangelism, and a biblical conception of health for the African church.[91]

In late July 1995, Dr. Zokoué returned to Bangui. After successfully defending his dissertation in Strasbourg, France, he took up his responsibilities as doyen once again. Leaving Bangui with Theo for North America and Europe in search of more funding for the seminary, we visited individuals, churches, and Christian agencies, from coast to coast in the United States, updating those who had expressed interest in FATEB's work of training leaders for African churches. We then made stops in England, the Netherlands, Germany, and France to visit organizations and individuals who had been assisting FATEB. These organizations were not only helping financially but were also praying and sending visiting professors to Bangui.

A Reformed Church pastor in the Netherlands, Henk de Jong, had come to FATEB six times over the previous ten years, to teach courses in Old Testament. He and his wife Betsy welcomed us into their home and invited several colleagues to meet us while we were there. One man who had just finished his doctoral studies in the Netherlands told us that he was

---

89. Nupanga Weanzana, letter to Jack Robinson, 12.11.95.

90. Paul Schmidt, letter to Jack Robinson, 12.12.95.

91. Students of FATEB, *Phos* (June 1995), BONKOUNGOU Victor, DANFA Youssouph, DIOUF Adama, FEGOUTO Andre, KOURSOU David, MOUSSA Bongoyok, SHOPO Mipangu.

coming to FATEB to teach. This was Dr. Benno van den Toren, whose name we had not heard before. But in January 1997, Benno, his wife Berdine, and their three boys moved to Bangui where Benno began teaching on the seminary faculty. The van den Torens and Dr. Judy Hill as expatriate professors have made invaluable contributions to FATEB students over more than two decades.[92]

In 1996, events surrounding FATEB in the capital city of Bangui overshadowed the internal activities of the seminary. In April 1996, an army revolt broke out in Bangui. The mutiny over unpaid salaries in the military began on Thursday, April 18. It included about 400 soldiers who commandeered private vehicles and clashed with loyalist troops. The issue of unpaid earnings had also caused teachers and other civil servants to go on strike earlier that week. France had 1,300 soldiers in the country, and they took control of major installations in Bangui on Saturday, April 20, crushing the army revolt, but only after 43 people had been killed and over 200 wounded.[93]

On Friday, April 26, the American embassy circulated a five-page paper to the American citizens in C.A.R., recommending that they remain in their homes or restrict movement until the local situation improved. The embassy further advised US citizens to leave C.A.R. if their presence was not essential.[94] Although relative calm had been reestablished by the French, it was clear that the reasons for the unrest had not been resolved and that further deterioration of the situation was possible.

Almost a month later, on Saturday morning, May 18, 1996, hostilities broke out once more between dissident army forces and the government. By evening, evacuation of foreigners had begun. On that same day, Dr. Zokoué and one of the students were an hour's drive out of the city at Bouali Falls, along with Dr. Benno van den Toren and two Dutch church officials who had come to see FATEB where Dr. van den Toren was planning to teach. While they were there, the roads into Bangui were closed by the insurrection, which left them stranded outside Bangui.

On Monday, May 20, Zokoué sent a request to the C.A.R. government to bring them back safely to Bangui. Though the government did not receive his communication, the next day Zokoué heard that a government

---

92. Jack Robinson, newsletter, January 1996.

93. Associated Press, "World News Briefs"; Jack Robinson, newsletter, October 1996.

94. United States Embassy, Possible embassy recommendations for U.S. citizens, 4.26.96.

helicopter was coming to Bouali. He managed to get to the local air strip in time to persuade the pilot to take van den Toren and the two Dutch church leaders to the national airport, so they could leave the country. Zokoué and the student who was with him then drove the school van back toward the capital. Barriers guarded by soldiers prevented them from getting closer to Bangui than 10 miles outside the city limits. So, they hid the school van and walked for several hours back to the campus. Zokoué discovered later that the helicopter that had taken the two Dutch visitors back to the Bangui airport had also been carrying the president of C.A.R. who had been on business in Bouali. That is why the helicopter had come to Bouali Falls that day.[95]

After six frightening days of listening to gunfire outside the campus and hearing stray bullets hitting the tin roofs on the campus, we and 14 other Americans and Europeans were taken to the airport in a French armored personnel carrier on May 23, 1996. The Americans were flown by American military transport to Yaoundé, capital of the neighboring country of Cameroon. Leaving our African colleagues and students behind to an uncertain future in Bangui was the hardest thing we had to face in this eruption of civil unrest. Dr. Zokoué later telephoned to inform us that the campus community had been protected from injuries by stray bullets and looters. The students and staff prayed and posted guards to protect the campus community all night long for the next two weeks. During the second week, the seminary was able to resume classes. With the evacuation of three faculty and two staff members, the remaining seminary professors were overloaded with work. They evaluated master's theses and taught extra classes to complete the school year by July 28, 1996. By God's grace, no soldiers or looters entered the FATEB campus grounds.[96]

1996-1997: STUDENTS GRADUATE DESPITE OUTBREAKS OF VIOLENCE

On September 16, 1996, FATEB began its twentieth academic year. With increased scholarship assistance, 18 new students enrolled, making a total of 57 men and women in the degree program from 13 African nations and many different church backgrounds. In addition, student spouses continued to receive three years of training in the Women's School. During our

95. John Bass, fax message, 5.22.96.
96. Jack Robinson, newsletters, July and October 1996.

travels in mid-1996, Theo and I visited fourteen FATEB alumni in five different countries: Zaire, Cameroon, Senegal, Côte d'Ivoire, and the USA. Of those whom we visited, nine men and one woman had completed the master's program, and four had finished the Women's School program. Of the master's graduates, three had begun serving as pastors, one was doing radio evangelism, another had founded an African mission society, one was directing denominational youth work, another was leading a national university student ministry, two were heads of pastoral training institutes, two others taught in pastoral training schools, and one had joined FATEB's faculty while pursuing a doctorate in the USA. Three of the four graduates of the Women's School were assisting their husbands and were focused on the evangelism and discipleship of women. The fourth worked with her husband in FATEB administration.[97]

A third army mutiny began on November 15, 1996, the weekend we were flying back to Bangui from the United States. Our flight stopped in England, and I phoned the American embassy in Bangui to ask their advice on our return. They said the situation was tense but calm, and they thought we could safely complete our trip to the capital. But by the first week of December, the embassy requested us to leave once more. The following week, a two-week truce was in place but was due to run out December 22, 1996. The rebels said they would renew fighting if the president did not resign. That, he refused to do. So, we five Americans, Paul and Phyllis Schmidt, Judy Hill, Theo, and I, flew out of Bangui just before the truce was scheduled to end in December.

On December 23, Zokoué sent us a fax message saying that a one-month extension to the truce had been negotiated. He reported that the Christmas celebration on campus that ended classes for 1996 had been held without incident. For that news we were grateful. Yet, uncertainty remained. Neither the students nor the professors wanted to leave the campus, and we wanted to return to FATEB as soon as it was safe to do so. Before flying out of Bangui in December, we participated with the campus community in daily periods of intense prayer for God's intervention in the country and for courage to carry on when we all felt we just wanted to hide.[98]

Classes resumed on January 6, 1997, with 90 percent of the students still there and all the African faculty and staff committed to carrying on.

---

97. Jack Robinson, newsletter, October 1996.

98. Isaac Zokoué, fax message to Jack Robinson, 12.23.96; Jack Robinson, newsletter, 1.2.97.

Everyone was in the process of learning more about how to be obedient to God in a world that seemed too full of violence and chaos. How the faculty and staff responded to this challenge would certainly have an impact on the students, many of whom would conduct much of their lives and ministries in contexts of civil fragility or disorder.[99]

On January 25, 1997, Dr. Zokoué sent an email message announcing that long negotiations with the chief of the military rebellion had ended with the signature of a ceasefire protocol that officially ended the mutiny in Bangui. The presidents of Gabon and Chad were present to witness the signing ceremony. Zokoué admitted that there was much to be done politically, militarily, socially, and religiously to heal the wounds of violence. But he expressed his gratitude to God for the end of the mutiny and the encouragement and prayers of so many people.[100] The ceasefire meant that if the conditions of the truce were applied, FATEB could continue its training ministry in peace, and we could return to Bangui in late March.[101]

Despite the peace agreement signed in late January, rebel soldiers refused to leave the parts of the city that they still controlled. By late March 1997, insecurity in the capital had become so severe that even the American embassy personnel left the country. More negotiations ended in mid-April with a public ceremony of reconciliation. The soldiers relinquished their military positions in the city and returned to their barracks. On May 8, 1997, we were able to fly into Bangui to take up our ministry there again. Throughout these first four months of 1997, the African professors, staff, and students kept moving ahead with classes, accompanied by much praise to God for his protection of them and the campus.

During one final political and military upheaval in 1997, from June 20 to 27, rebel troops attacked the United Nations African peacekeepers in Bangui. Over the previous 15 months, at least 500 civilians were killed and 70,000 driven from their homes. In this June 1997 attack, three mortars exploded near the FATEB grounds, a stray bullet lodged in the leg of a student on campus, and three students lost relatives in clashes off campus. That confrontation marked the end of a season of public violence, and general calm in the capital city of Bangui reigned for the rest of the calendar year.

The FATEB board of directors had met in May 1997 and expressed strong interest in adding more qualified African professors to the faculty.

---

99. Jack Robinson, letter to friends, 1.2.97.
100. Isaac Zokoué, fax message to Jack Robinson, 1.25.97.
101. Jack Robinson, email to Isaac Zokoué, 1.31.97.

After five months of absence, expatriate professors were gradually returning to campus. Despite the difficult conditions in the capital, ten students from Burkina Faso, Zaire, Rwanda, and Central African Republic finished their master's programs.

A dependable water supply was lacking on campus, but the drilling of a well was successfully completed toward the end of the 1996–1997 school year. What remained to be done was the installation of a pump and the construction of a modest water tower on campus.

Daniel Mangonda, who had graduated from FATEB in 1995, finished four months of specialized training in Abidjan, Côte d'Ivoire, to become FATEB's next librarian. With a library of over 13,000 books and the construction of a new library building scheduled to begin in the near future, Daniel's work would be important to the faculty and students.

The FATEB community was looking forward to graduation in July 1997 and the celebration of its 20-year anniversary of classes. In June, Nupanga, the vice-doyen, completed a report to FATEB friends, acknowledging the special difficulties of the past year but thanking God for his faithfulness and requesting friends of the seminary to continue supporting the community with their prayers.[102]

Graduation that July was an unusually joyful event as the campus community had prayed together and helped one another in the times of common danger throughout the school year. Deep bonds of unity were evident as the graduates and their families said goodbye, leaving for their respective churches in the countries from which they had come. Strong emotional ties would remain as they pursued common goals for strengthening the African churches.[103]

1997–1998: FATEB UNDERTAKES NEW PROJECTS DURING A YEAR OF PEACE

Good news accompanied the approach of the new academic year. Almost $60,000 in grants of financial assistance were made to 34 of the new and returning students, making a positive impact on the enrollment of the seminary.

---

102. Nupanga Weanzana, newsletter to FATEB friends, 6.15.97; Jack Robinson, newsletter, 6.13.97.

103. United States Embassy, Excerpt from a Central African Republic Country Report on Human Rights Practices for 1997; Jack Robinson, newsletter, 8.8.97.

Early Leaders—Josaphat Paluku, Isaac Zokoué

In March 1996, Evangelical Free Church missionaries Ken and Judy Landrud, serving in Zaire, had expressed their interest in FATEB's new library construction project. Landrud, a skilled builder, had been managing building programs for African churches and the Tandala mission hospital in northwestern Zaire. Deciding to relocate in Bangui to begin building FATEB's library, the Landruds had waited for a year and a half, until September 1997, to make their move to C.A.R.'s capital. By October of 1997, Landrud had construction under way. With the library collection having grown to 14,000 volumes, its location on the second floor of the classroom building risked collapsing the entire structure from the weight of the book stacks. The new facility would devote an entire floor to the growing library and provide study space for the students as well.[104]

Plans for the new library under construction showed a three-level building with the library on the top floor, faculty offices on the second floor, and a large multipurpose area on the ground floor that would seat several hundred people. Overseas Council, based in Indianapolis, Indiana, USA, was providing major funding, and library completion was scheduled for 1999.[105]

In the 1997–1998 school year, 76 students were enrolled at FATEB. By this time, the curriculum had been divided into a three-year bachelor's degree program and a two-year master's degree program. Assisted by the new scholarship fund, 54 students had enrolled in the degree programs and 22 students in the Women's School. The student body came from 11 different French-speaking African countries. The students produced another edition of *Phos* that was devoted to the challenge of tribalism in Africa. Five of the students and the vice-doyen wrote articles for it. The African Theological Initiative (ATI), which offers financial resources to church leadership training institutions in Africa, named FATEB a "model institution." FATEB was noted for its library, conferences, faculty exchange, management training, and publications.[106]

In January of 1998, faculty and key administrators met to review position descriptions, student recruitment, academic curriculum, student internships, progress on the search for additional faculty and staff, professor workloads, electronic equipment, and the doctoral program scheduled to begin later that year. A doctoral commission met to discuss access to

---

104. Ken Landrud, letter to Jack Robinson, 3.9.96; Jack Robinson, newsletter, 10.21.97.
105. Jack Robinson, notes on construction plans, 1.27.98.
106. Jack Robinson, newsletter, 4.15.98.

libraries outside of Africa, to evaluate professor qualifications for the programs, ensure contextualization of the studies, review rationale and objectives for the doctoral program at FATEB, agree on criteria and prerequisites for admission, and consider partnership with other schools.[107]

As for C.A.R. itself, another step toward national peace was taken in March 1998, when a formal reconciliation was signed by representatives of the government, military, labor, religious groups, and the major political parties. Dr. Zokoué, FATEB's doyen, had been chosen by the 300 delegates to preside over the week-long conference. Five heads of state from neighboring countries, along with representatives of other government organizations and many Central Africans, came to witness the pledges. The president publicly thanked God for his gracious help in bringing an end to the hostilities and restoring peace. To ensure the preservation of peace, the United Nations decided to maintain a military peace-keeping presence in C.A.R. for the coming months.[108]

In April 1998, FATEB welcomed to campus 100 pastors from C.A.R. and neighboring D.R. Congo for a conference on "The Renewal of the Pastoral Ministry." The pastor's personal life and public responsibilities were addressed. This conference was organized as part of FATEB's 20-year anniversary celebration.[109]

In July 1998, FATEB held its annual graduation ceremonies after an entire year of relative calm. No classes had been canceled for lack of security under the sound of gunfire in the city. Yet, some of the graduates were returning to troubled countries. For two families, one from Rwanda and the other from Burundi, going back home into a context of extreme ethnic hostility was to risk considerable danger. According to one reliable source, over 60 percent of the Evangelical Christian leaders in Rwanda disappeared between April 1994 and February 1997. The very churches that sent these students to FATEB were encouraging them not to return because of fear for their lives. The churches, however, would need their leadership in the years ahead, as the wounds of genocide were still in need of healing.[110]

---

107. Jack Robinson, newsletter, 4.15.98.

108. Jack Robinson, newsletter, 4.15.98; Jack Robinson, report on the national reconciliation in Central African Republic, 3.16.98.

109. Jack Robinson, newsletter, 4.15.98.

110. Jack Robinson, newsletter, 7.15.98.

Early Leaders—Josaphat Paluku, Isaac Zokoué

1998–1999: CONFLICTS IN BORDERING COUNTRIES IMPACT STUDENTS AT FATEB

In October 1998, the new school year began with the addition of thirteen new students in the degree programs and seven more women enrolling in the Women's School. The student body represented 12 French-speaking countries. Two African professors with doctorates also joined the faculty in September, with two more expected in another year.[111] Additionally, Dr. David Koudougueret, a member of FATEB's first graduating class, became academic dean of FATEB.

Paul Schmidt, FATEB's certified public accountant, fully computerized the financial accounting system. He also trained a capable African to take over his job. Dr. Zokoué embarked on a seven-month sabbatical in South Africa, preparing his doctoral research on the Person of Christ for publication, to be used as a textbook in French-speaking Africa.[112]

Even though C.A.R. had experienced 18 months of peace by the end of 1998, the civil war that had begun in the neighboring Zaire in October 1996 (renamed the Democratic Republic of Congo in 1997) deeply impacted the students at FATEB. Bangui is separated from northwest Congo by the Ubangi River, and many of the seminary students and staff had parents, siblings, and Christian friends living in that area of Congo. Dr. Nupanga wrote to say that his hometown of Gemena had been retaken by government soldiers, opening the way to savage reprisal killings of rebels. He wrote, "I don't know what has happened to my father and my five brothers who could easily be mistaken for rebels." By then, soldiers from six other countries had been drawn into the conflict. Just the previous week, 43 refugees from Nupanga's home area in Congo had arrived on his doorstep in Bangui asking for help. The seminary was housing refugees from the Congolese churches and trying to find continuing shelter for them. With heavy hearts for those suffering in this nearby country, the FATEB community was experiencing more of what it means to live as faithful servants of Christ during terrible social, political, military, and economic upheaval.[113]

In the midst of this widespread insecurity, students were going to classes. In April 1999, second-year students were taking exams in church history. Sitting between two pastors from Bangui, Eveline, a gifted woman

---

111. Jack Robinson, newsletter, November 1998.
112. Jack Robinson, newsletter, November 1998.
113. Jack Robinson, newsletter, January 1999.

from Cameroon, married to the student body president and expecting their first baby, was writing her exam. Near her was Lillian from Kinshasa, Congo. Married to another student in the class, Lillian had made outstanding progress. A treasury inspector and former congressman was bending over his exam paper, trying to recall discussions on how Christ's church had unfolded over the centuries. Each student represented a potential for leadership in the African churches. It was for them and their future ministries that this seminary had been founded.[114]

By the end of the 1998–1999 school year, graduates of the master's program had defended their theses before a three-member jury. A student from Rwanda had written his thesis on how Christians in his culture should face death in a context of war and tribal conflict. Another student wrote about how the congregations in his country could participate in the missionary outreach of the church. In addition to evaluating theses, completing courses, and giving exams, professors visited churches to see how students were doing in their internships, helped decide on the admission of students for the new school year, assisted students with financial aid requests, and communicated with individuals and churches abroad who supported the seminary.

In 1999, the faculty decided to begin visiting FATEB alumni in their home countries to encourage them in their ministries and to report back to FATEB their suggestions for improving learning opportunities at the seminary. The doyen asked Theo and me to visit six countries in French Africa in the following year to help carry out this plan.[115]

1999–2000: THREE-STORY CONSTRUCTION SUPERVISED BY MISSIONARY KEN LANDRUD

In November 1999, the FATEB community celebrated the end of a large construction project that had taken two years to complete. The original idea had been to construct a proper library, but the plans had evolved into what the doyen called an academic complex. Here is the way Dr. Nupanga described it:

> If you were to walk through the entrance to FATEB's campus today for the first time, your eyes would be drawn to the structure at the

---

114. Jack Robinson, newsletter, April 1999.
115. Jack Robinson, newsletter, June 1999.

end of the driveway directly in front of you. Three stories high, cream colored with burnt red trim, the building invites visitors to walk under graceful arches and into the first-floor conference center through mahogany wood doors made from Central African Republic's rich tropical rain forest. Over 400 people filled the assembly hall on November 7th for the inauguration of the entire complex. Following the ceremony, government ministers, foreign ambassadors and international guests went up to the third floor where the 15,000 books of the Byang Kato library are arranged and where study carrels, a spacious reading room and library offices are located overlooking the entire campus. Refreshments were served on the second floor in the three conference rooms next to the eight faculty offices. It was a proud day for the Central African skilled laborers who constructed this complex under the direction of missionary builder, Ken Landrud. All of us at FATEB express our heartfelt thanks to Overseas Council International whose generous financial support helped make this facility possible.[116]

This new building would serve students and faculty for years to come.

In July 1999, a record graduating class of 17 students from the degree programs and the Women's School completed their studies at FATEB. Several graduating families left to return to countries stricken by genocide and civil war. One family returned to Rwanda; two families to the former French Congo where there had been civil war for over two years; and four families returned to the D.R. Congo. Each of these countries was suffering terribly. The conditions of life and work were dangerous in these young nations under military rule and troubled by rebel soldiers. The graduates were commended to God as they left FATEB for their homes amid political, military, and economic turmoil to face daunting challenges ahead.[117]

A new class of students entered FATEB in October 1999, and two graduates returned to FATEB from advanced studies to assume full-time teaching duties. Dr. Mavinga came to teach Old Testament, and Moussa Bongoyok, with his passion for Islamic studies, began teaching missiology. Progress was being made in reclaiming the adjoining five acres of property still occupied by some city families. The land was greatly needed for faculty and student housing. United Nations peacekeepers had helped keep the peace in C.A.R. for the previous two and a half years. As the millennium ended, the FATEB community was rejoicing in God's faithfulness and

---

116. Isaac Zokoué, FATEB president's report, November 1999.
117. Isaac Zokoué, FATEB president's report, November 1999.

feeling optimistic about the future. The school could look back over significant development. FATEB had grown in student enrollment, in African faculty, and in financial support and had added a beautiful building with a library, an assembly hall, and faculty offices. There was much for which to give thanks.[118]

In March 2000, Theo and I began a series of annual visits to alumni of FATEB living in the francophone countries of west and central Africa. We made a long trip to six west African countries from March 9 to May 31, 2000. The aim was to encourage FATEB graduates by visits to their places of ministry, to listen to them, and to pray with them about the challenges they were facing in their lives and ministries. In addition, information was needed from them that might help to strengthen FATEB's training programs. On each visit, the alumni were asked about their ministry responsibilities, about critical issues facing African churches, about what had been most helpful in their training at FATEB, and about suggestions they could offer to FATEB. They shared requests for prayer, and we recorded our own observations as well as other useful comments made by those whom we visited. Upon returning to Bangui in June 2000, we shared this information with the faculty and staff of the seminary. We had also made a short video of each couple with advice they wanted to pass along to those still in training. Students in Bangui watched and listened to the videos with rapt attention. These reports represented important evaluations of FATEB's effectiveness in the lives of those whom the school was equipping for ministry.[119]

---

118. Jack Robinson, newsletter, February 2000.
119. Jack Robinson, trip report, 2000.

CHAPTER 5

Broadening the Vision—Abel Ndjéraréou, Nupanga Weanzana

2000–2001: TRAINING IN BIBLE TRANSLATION ADDED TO FATEB'S CURRICULUM

The major change at FATEB in the year 2000 was the completion of Dr. Isaac Zokoué's fourteenth year as doyen and the appointment of his successor, Dr. Abel Ndjéraréou, of Chad.

D<small>R. N<small>DJÉRARÉOU HAD COMPLETED</small></small> his doctoral studies in Old Testament at Dallas Theological Seminary, USA, in 1995. He then served as director of Chad's Shalom Evangelical Graduate School of Theology (ESTES) and also served as the president of the Evangelical Church of Chad. Dr. Ndjéraréou had taught at FATEB as a visiting professor many times over the previous decade. He assumed his responsibilities as doyen of FATEB on September 1, 2000.[1]

Two months before this leadership change, a strategic planning process was initiated in July 2000 under the direction of the vice-chairman of the board of governors, Jonas Bebongo, and assisted by retiring Doyen Zokoué. The aim was to map out the executive staff's consensus on where FATEB was headed in the coming years and how it would get there.

An updated mission statement of FATEB was affirmed:

---

1. FATEB, "Press Release: New President at Bangui Evangelical Graduate School," September 2000.

> FATEB's mission is to contribute to the personal and theological development of men and women preparing for church leadership responsibilities in Africa through programs at multiple academic levels (doctoral, master's, bachelor's, diploma) designed to result in ministries that will assist African Christians to mature as disciples of Christ and to participate in fulfilling the mission to the world given by Jesus Christ to his Church.[2]

Those involved in the strategic planning process anticipated the following challenges that in the coming decade would be present in the African context: The advance of Islam, African traditional religion, "Christian" sects, the moral and intellectual impact of modernity, and social problems of great magnitude—poverty, disease, and ethnic tensions.

Addressing the needs of African churches would include educational programs that offered excellence in biblical and theological training, initiatives designed to develop Christian ethics, personal spiritual maturity that would translate the values of the gospel into life and ministry, and skills development in various disciplines needed by the churches. These capabilities would include communications and missions, youth ministries, Christian education, Bible translation, ministry in Islamic contexts, leadership, and management.

Essential values to be nurtured included faithfulness to God and the Scriptures in all that is done, servant-leadership, academic rigor, spiritual depth, moral integrity, ministerial competence, international cooperation, and diversity in ethnicity, nationality, church affiliation, and gender. The strategic plan went on to define objectives in ten different areas of FATEB's key sectors of activity.[3]

At the graduation ceremonies in July 2000, 18 men and women were granted degrees, and students who had completed the Women's School program received diplomas. Many would return to home countries torn by civil wars and social unrest to put into practice what they had learned.

Student enrollment set a record in the year 2000. The seminary received 56 new students, of whom 17 enrolled in the Women's School. Added to those already enrolled, the student body came to a total of 114. Many new students were housed temporarily off campus in the hope that

---

2. Isaac Zokoué, Strategic Planning—July 2000, 1.
3. Isaac Zokoué, Strategic Planning—July 2000, 1–2.

funds would become available for additional student housing construction on campus.[4]

All during the calendar year of 2001, Pastor Jean Jacques Nimézéambi, a mature FATEB graduate and member of FATEB's board, negotiated the departure of 66 individuals or families who had been sold land fraudulently on the undeveloped five acres that FATEB had received from the government ten years earlier and then temporarily lost. With these five acres and the initial government grant of seven acres, FATEB's campus encompassed a total of twelve acres. By November 20, 2001, all the occupants had signed departure contracts. The original cost of the negotiations had been estimated at around $150,000, of which Tyndale House Foundation financed two-thirds of the cost.[5] In the end, it cost $116,000 to complete the clearing of the five acres of land, not counting the additional expense of a security wall to enclose it.[6] Repossessing FATEB's land opened the way for new construction of greatly needed faculty housing.

Adding to FATEB's growth in a different arena, in January 2001 FATEB signed an agreement with SIL, the Wycliffe Bible Translators international organization, to provide training for national Bible translators. Two years of studies would be required under the teaching of FATEB professors in biblical languages and theology and under SIL personnel who were translation specialists. African translators would graduate with a general university degree in Bible translation and be able to work on the translation of the Scriptures into any of the many ethnic languages in central African countries approved for such a project. The United Bible Society also cooperated with FATEB in this project, and 11 new students enrolled in the program for their first year of training.[7]

Several conferences were held on FATEB's campus in 2001, including a conference on the biblical understanding of authority. Dr. Zokoué supervised the conference that included lectures by six speakers on related themes: "Authority in African Tradition," Dr. Kosse Kuzuli; "Theology and Practice of Authority in Islam," Dr. Moussa Bongoyok; "Authority in the Ancient Near East and Old Testament," Dr. Paul Mpindi; "Theology and the

---

4. Isaac Zokoué, FATEB president's report, December 2000; and FATEB president's report, April 2001, student total revised from 111 to 114.

5. Jack Robinson, newsletter, January 2001.

6. Floyd Bruning, letter to Jack Robinson, 10.1.01.

7. Isaac Zokoué, FATEB president's report, April 2001; David Koudougueret, faculty report, April 2001.

Practice of Authority in the New Testament," Dr. Judy Hill; "The Christian God and Human Authority," Dr. Benno van den Toren; "Church Authority," Dr. Enoch Tompté.

The women of FATEB met for a conference on February 13 to hear presentations by Dr. Judy Hill on unity within the FATEB community, and from Dr. Ndjéraréou and Chaplain Kuzuli on Christian life in multicultural community. Follow up discussions on "Women in Ministry in an African Context" were planned for March 31, 2001.[8]

Irma Janzon, wife of Dr. Göran Janzon, a regular visiting Swedish professor at FATEB, brought a delegation of 12 people from InterAct in Sweden to FATEB in January of 2001. To complete FATEB's self-sustaining water system that began in 1997 with the drilling of a campus well, funding was needed for the construction of a campus water tower. The visit of this delegation led to a commitment by InterAct to fund the project.[9]

Expatriate and visiting professors had assisted with the academic programs over many years at FATEB, and by 2001 eight resident African professors were teaching on campus. Nupanga Weanzana, who had been serving as vice-doyen since 1995, and who was in Pretoria, South Africa, in 2001 working on his doctorate in Old Testament, planned to return to the campus to teach. The work of the African professors helped to ensure that the seminary's program of studies would be suited to the needs of the African churches.[10]

Visits to graduates of FATEB in their various countries of work continued to offer insight into the effectiveness of FATEB training. In the Democratic Republic of Congo, visits were made to 15 alumni families. There, two FATEB graduates were serving as presidents of their Protestant denominations, another was serving as director of the Congo Bible Society, and a couple was giving conferences on marital and family life enrichment as well as training others to do the same. Both women and men were found serving as pastors. Other graduates had engaged in university student ministry.

In June of 2001, Theo and I visited FATEB alumni in the Republic of Congo, a former French colony across the Congo River from the D.R. Congo. It had suffered three civil wars in the previous eight years. The third of these conflicts had taken place in 1998–1999. Thousands of civilians had

---

8. Isaac Zokoué, FATEB president's report, April 2001.
9. Isaac Zokoué, FATEB president's report, April 2001.
10. David Koudougueret, faculty report, April 2001.

been killed in the fighting, and many more had fled into the tropical forest. Since 11 FATEB graduates and their families had returned to their homes there, the FATEB community was concerned about them and encouraged us to visit these alumni.[11]

Before arriving in Brazzaville, capital city of the Republic of Congo, we didn't realize how many of the civilian deaths had resulted from intentional ethnic killing, nor were we aware of the widespread looting and destruction of people's homes. During two weeks in the Republic of Congo, we learned much of what it had been like for the graduates to live through this horror. Now, they were trying to help people in their congregations heal from the trauma of losing all their material possessions and many loved ones. Trauma showed in their eyes as they related the almost unspeakable stories of cruelty.[12]

Boniface Yidika had graduated from FATEB in 1995. He was a senior pastor in the Evangelical Church of Congo, overseeing ten parishes and their pastors in Brazzaville. Tall, slim, energetic, and usually smiling broadly, this man in his forties had served his church through two civil wars since his graduation from FATEB. His wife, Isabel, had taken the lead in raising their four lovely girls and three active boys whose ages ranged from three to twenty-one. When we visited them, 18 months had passed since the war ended, but recollections of war experiences punctuated nearly every conversation. In one terrifying incident, the entire family had been forced to their knees with guns to their heads, ready to be executed. At the last instant, a soldier of higher rank walked into the room where they were kneeling and prevented them from being killed. The family was still trying to heal from this trauma.[13]

How do Christians respond to such human cruelty? Isaac Locko, a retired judge and the father of a FATEB graduate from Brazzaville, Serge Locko, recounted a moving story of forgiveness by his brother's children after the murder of their father. At the sight of his murdered brother, Judge Locko said to the children, "Now we must forgive the people who did this." And kneeling to pray, they did so. Serge Locko said to us, "Today, eight years later, the children are doing well."[14]

---

11. Jack Robinson, newsletter, January 2001.
12. Jack Robinson, newsletter, January 2001.
13. Jack Robinson, newsletter, January 2001.
14. Jack Robinson, newsletter, January 2001.

Other graduates serving in the former French Congo were carrying out ministries adapted to the challenges of post-war recovery there: ministries to widows, orphans, street kids, and elderly people without families. One couple had started a medical center in their church to assist those unable to pay for health care. Others were engaged in adult literacy, self-help development projects, and reconstruction of damaged and looted buildings. Our listening to their experiences and praying for their concerns helped them realize that Christians outside their country cared about them and had not forgotten them.[15]

In late May 2001, a coup d'état was attempted in C.A.R., though it failed to overturn the government. Despite this major disruption in civilian life, on July 15, 18 FATEB students received their degrees and then left the campus to be reintegrated into the countries from which they had come. They became part of over 300 graduates of FATEB scattered throughout central and west Africa.

2001-2002: TRAUMA WORKSHOPS ORGANIZED

In July 2001, Paul Schmidt, who had served as FATEB's financial manager since January 1996, returned to the United States. His decision to leave had been precipitated by the unwillingness of FATEB leadership to respect the seminary's budgetary financial limits on spending. Floyd Bruning, a retired certified public accountant who had been assisting with FATEB's accounting from his base in North America, traveled to Bangui in September 2001 to help with FATEB's accounting needs following Schmidt's departure. Bruning completed the financial report for FATEB's 2000–2001 fiscal year, which ended August 31. To his surprise, Bruning discovered that the operating deficit for the previous year had surpassed $100,000 (79,000,000 CFA). This was a terrible shock and a reflection of the flawed financial management Schmidt had warned about. Long meetings were held to determine how to minimize the projected deficit for the 2001–2002 fiscal year. Bruning provided the doyen with four different cost-cutting financial analyses showing how the next year could end at a financial break-even point.[16]

---

15. Jack Robinson, newsletter, January 2001.

16. Jack Robinson, letter to Manfred Kohl, late 2001; Floyd Bruning, letter to Abel Ndjéraréou, 12.3.01.

A group of new students began arriving in September 2001. The administration struggled to find the additional housing and operating funds needed to sustain this growing student community.[17] Student enrollment had more than doubled from what it had been two years earlier. The five acres of FATEB's property on the southern border of the current seven-acre campus had at last been vacated, and the new property had been completely enclosed and secured, ready for the building of additional faculty housing. The political upheavals of the previous year, with periods of fighting in the capital city early in the year, had been followed with calm and a greater sense of unity among the general population.[18]

The preparation of students at FATEB for church ministries did not include specific training in how to help people traumatized by the civil wars and violence experienced by many civilians. One way that FATEB was able to address such needs was through workshops. In April of 2002, Dr. Frances White, a former D.R. Congo missionary who had taught psychology at Wheaton College (USA) for twenty years, came to Bangui to do a four-day trauma workshop for the students. Earlier in 2002 she had conducted training sessions in the former French Congo for pastors and lay leaders in how to help people suffering from severe and persistent trauma resulting from the civil wars there. About 60 students participated in the FATEB workshop in Bangui, grateful to understand how to assist those who needed healing of the spirit from the wounds of humanity's inhumanity.[19]

As always, the student body of FATEB represented a diversity of nationalities, ethnicities, and church denominations. But the regions from which the students came reflected different religious contexts. The eight francophone countries in central Africa had Christian majorities, tending to be more Catholic than Protestant. Islam was more prevalent in the eight francophone countries of west Africa, being the majority religion in most of those nations. Because FATEB received students from those countries with Muslim majorities, the faculty and administration decided to organize a conference on Muslim ministry in May of 2002. They hoped to add to the master's curriculum a new major in ministry to Muslims. They wanted students to be prepared to minister to the spiritually needy of any religious background, including Muslims.[20]

17. Jack Robinson, newsletter, October 2001.
18. Jack Robinson, newsletter, January 2002.
19. Jack Robinson, newsletters, April and June, 2002.
20. Jack Robinson, newsletter, January 2002.

An African Dream

FATEB graduate Moussa Bongoyok was born and raised in the strongly Muslim area of northern Cameroon. He grew up speaking Fulfulde, the language of the Fulani people. Between 17 and 20 million nomadic Fulani people lived in west and central Africa. Only a small minority had had any significant contact with Christianity. During the 2001–2002 school year, Bongoyok was engaged in Islamic studies at Fuller School of World Mission, preparing to further develop a program at FATEB to train people for ministry in Muslim contexts. Since Islam was the largest non-Christian religious group in Africa, FATEB leaders wanted to see this program launched.[21]

Faculty members were consciously equipping men and women at the seminary for mission outreach in their respective countries. Younoussa and Alphonsine Djao both graduated from the master's program at FATEB in 1996 and returned to their home country, Côte d'Ivoire. Djao was active in promoting biannual regional consultations on evangelizing unreached peoples in west and central Africa. In 2002, over 300 people attended the third of these conferences in Abidjan. This five-day meeting focused on how to partner with one another in advancing the missionary task of the church. Also attending the conference were many African missionaries sent by newly organized African mission agencies.

In addition to Djao's contributions at the conference, his wife Alphonsine gave a passionate address, pleading that African cultural restrictions be put aside to allow African Christian women to participate fully in the missionary task. She confronted the listeners with the fact that 86 percent of the yet unreached people in west Africa were women and children. In that context, this population could only be effectively reached by women. It was inspiring and encouraging to see the Djaos at the conference and to meet 12 FATEB graduates, both men and women, who were filling significant roles in mission initiatives of the churches.[22]

2002–2003: GOVERNMENT COUP D'ÉTAT, FATEB SECURITY COMPROMISED

As 2003 began, FATEB was still struggling financially after the end of the difficult 2001–2002 fiscal year. The economic downturn in the United States in late 2002 and the sharp rise in food costs because of rebel blockades of routes into Bangui created financial problems for the campus community.

21. Jack Robinson, newsletter, November 2002.
22. Jack Robinson, newsletter, June 2002.

United Nations peace-keeping forces from other countries were having only marginal success in their mission.[23] The political issues in C.A.R. were translating into military conflict and grew out of rebels' attempts to overthrow the government.[24] Regional and ethnic tensions between the people living in the northern part of C.A.R. and those in the south who controlled most of the political and economic power in the country fueled the conflict.

On March 15, 2003, while the C.A.R. president, Patassé, was out of the country, General François Bozizé organized a successful coup and became C.A.R.'s chief of state. Looting was widespread and intense, and the security of the FATEB campus was breached. Vehicles and saleable equipment were taken. One of the staff children was kidnapped by a soldier, and only the payment of a ransom prevented the loss of the child. The campus community lived through great anxiety. Gradually, order was restored in the capital, and the vehicles were returned. Although classes eventually resumed, it would take time for normalcy to truly return. Bozizé's coup ended what had been six months of civil war within the country.[25]

In July 2003, about 40 men and women completed various programs leading to master's and bachelor's degrees, diplomas from the Women's School, and certificates for those finishing a two-year program in Bible translation. Security seemed adequate, the government had begun paying salaries, and the local citizens were cautiously optimistic about the future of the country.

2003–2004: FINANCIAL CRISIS, BUT RESCUE BY GENEROUS FRIENDS

February 2004 marked the halfway point in the 2003–2004 school year. For Evangelical studies, biblical English language materials were especially important. With many of FATEB's biblical library resources in English, classes in theological English assisted students to make good use of the library's English language books and periodicals. Students also studied the early church fathers, among them African church leaders such as Cyprian, Athanasius, and Augustine. These theologians of the third and fourth centuries still influence the understanding of Christians today about what

---

23. Jack Robinson, newsletter, January 2003.

24. Jack Robinson, newsletter, March 2003.

25. Jack Robinson, newsletters, May and August 2003; see Wikipedia, "2003 Central African Republic Coup d'Etat"; and Wikipedia, "François Bozizé."

the Bible teaches concerning God, humanity, and salvation. One student asked: "Why did you wait until our last year before telling us about these great men?" He had discovered the rich spiritual heritage in these early Christians and realized for the first time that outstanding Africans figured among the church fathers.[26]

Outside the seminary in 2004, the capital city had been peaceful since the military coup in March of 2003. Dr. Zokoué, FATEB's former doyen, had again been asked to preside over nationwide reconciliation discussions among political factions as he had done once before. National elections were scheduled for January 2005. Until democratic elections were held, the American embassy would not reopen. Citizens hoped that elections would end a turbulent decade and begin a durable peace in the Central African Republic.[27]

While progress was being made nationally, FATEB was facing one of the worst financial crises of its 27-year history. The weakening US dollar, the increase in operating expenses, the employment of qualified nationals who, in contrast to foreign missionaries, had to be paid by the school, and the inability of African churches to shoulder much of the training costs all contributed to the crisis. By mid-February 2004, city water to the campus had been turned off for almost two months because of unpaid water bills. Public faucets located off campus became the source of washing and drinking water, transported in buckets on women's heads as in the past. The doyen did not know how he would pay salaries in the months until new tuition money would arrive for the 2004–2005 school year. After almost three years of searching for a replacement since the departure of FATEB's previous financial manager, a qualified Kenyan, Joe Mwangi, certified public accountant, arrived at FATEB to direct the financial affairs of the school.[28] Mwangi's work significantly improved FATEB's financial accounting, but it did not arrest the annual deficit spending approved by the doyen.

City water was turned on again at FATEB in March 2004. Security improved. The seminary salaries were not paid that month; by May 2004 over $50,000 had been contributed from concerned supporters to keep the seminary functioning. An American friend mortgaged her home to be able

---

26. Jack Robinson, newsletter, 2.18.04.
27. Jack Robinson, newsletter, 2.18.04.
28. Jack Robinson, newsletter, 2.18.04.

to help FATEB in a substantial way. Because of such unexpected gifts, progress toward financial stability was gradually taking place.[29]

In July of 2004, graduating students finished their studies at FATEB and returned to their churches and ministries in many different countries in Africa. A couple from Rwanda was invited to serve in the Reformed Church in Tunisia. The Tunisian church had sent Rwandan Jean Nzabarushimana to FATEB for training five years earlier. During the Rwandan genocide, he had fled to Tunisia as a refugee. While in Bangui, Jean had married a Rwandan woman, and together they returned to Tunisia to serve there.[30]

2004–2005: DOCTORAL PROGRAM LAUNCHED; NEW BUILDINGS FOR THE PRIMARY SCHOOL

Life in Africa could be tragically short. In 2004, in Abidjan, Côte d'Ivoire, one of FATEB's graduates from the class of 1992, Blaise Gawa, died suddenly. Gawa was praying with one of his parishioners when he suddenly collapsed and died of an apparent heart attack. He was 48 years old and had been head of a Bible school in western Côte d'Ivoire for eight years. To lose this respected and competent church leader was a shock to all who knew him.[31]

Continuing education for faculty members at FATEB was important to maintaining relevant instruction in a rapidly changing world. A weeklong Forum for World Evangelization was held in Thailand in late September and early October 2004, on the thirtieth anniversary of the well-known Lausanne Congress of 1974. Over 1,500 participants from 130 countries gathered to seek guidance for churches around the world in carrying out their evangelistic mission. Several faculty members from FATEB were at the forum and then returned to Bangui to report to faculty and students what they had learned. Topics of the forum included the state of non-Christian religions; terrorism; the need for reconciliation in a hostile world; the plight of the world's children, youth, and others at risk; the persecuted church; political and religious nationalism; and the challenge of HIV. The consensus of the forum group discussing the equipping of future leaders for the church was that what was needed most was not more leaders, or even

---

29. Jack Robinson, newsletter, 5.12.04.
30. Jack Robinson, newsletter, 7.26.04.
31. Jack Robinson, newsletter, 8.18.04.

more competent leaders, but leaders who were more like Jesus, a message the delegates were charged to share with their home countries.[32]

Between 1992 and 2005, the primary school on campus continued to receive children from families in the city in addition to children of the FATEB students. By 2005, the number of children who were attending the FATEB primary school had outgrown its existing campus facilities. The earliest primary school classrooms had been built on the original campus next to the men's dormitory. In 2005, additional primary school buildings were constructed on the new five acres south of the older seven-acre campus. To meet the need for additional faculty and staff housing, two multifamily residences were also completed on the new property. FATEB friends in Europe and North America had helped financially to make these expanded facilities possible.[33]

After years of planning, FATEB's doctoral program was inaugurated in January 2005. Its founding purpose was to equip those planning to lead other training institutions at advanced levels in their respective francophone countries. Dr. Zokoué headed this initiative. Resident African and expatriate professors in Bangui, along with visiting professors from Europe and North America, provided instruction for the doctoral students.[34]

Nearly 30 men and women graduated from FATEB in July of 2005. The school year was undisturbed by political unrest. A national presidential run-off election proceeded smoothly, and the capital city of Bangui was calm, though life remained difficult economically.[35]

2005–2006: TEAM FROM WHEATON BIBLE CHURCH DOES CAMPUS RENOVATIONS

In early 2006, a team of three women and seven men from Wheaton Bible Church (USA) came to FATEB for almost two weeks to assist with several campus renovation projects. The FATEB community was amazed that so large a team of Christians had traveled so far to this little-known French-speaking country to help for so long. The team members not only upgraded

---

32. Jack Robinson, newsletter, 10.9.04.
33. Jack Robinson, newsletter, 2.24.05.
34. Jack Robinson, newsletter, 2.24.05.
35. Jack Robinson, newsletter, 7.14.05.

and beautified various campus buildings but also expressed to students and staff their concern and love.[36]

The Women's School was the major focus of the visiting team's work. FATEB graduates have consistently rated FATEB's training of student wives for ministry as one of its most valued contributions. The original single-level frame building on campus became the home for women's training when administrative functions and degree programs were moved to other campus buildings. The Bible Church team created a computer training lab with eight computer stations. They also built a louvered wall to separate the major Women's School classroom from the rest of the school where sewing and cooking classes were conducted. A nearby thatched-roof nursery was enlarged and reroofed. This facility cared for the babies of the mothers while they were attending classes. Three preschool classrooms were repainted and decorated with educational art. The large hall used for chapel and conferences in the multipurpose building was given an artistic rendering of the school's motto, and key biblical texts were painted on the interior walls to keep the values and mission of the seminary visible. One of the ways the Women's School students showed their appreciation for these visitors was to sew African shirts for each team member. This visiting group was long remembered by the African students and staff at FATEB.[37]

2006–2007: MINISTRY TO MUSLIMS TRAINING

A specialization in the master's level program designed to prepare men and women for ministry in Islamic environments in Africa was begun in September 2006 and led by FATEB graduate Dr. Moussa Bongoyok. FATEB leaders understood that many people in the world demonized Muslims, as in the tragedy of the Crusades of the twelfth and thirteenth centuries. Such an approach did not attract people to Christ or bring healing to those traumatized by the religious hostilities that had torn the world apart. Bongoyok understood that such hostility did not reflect the ethics of Jesus who instructed his followers to forgive their brothers and love their enemies. This missiology program aimed to help Christian leaders in Africa to speak and live the radical love of God who cares for the world and longs for people to be reconciled to himself.[38]

36. Jack Robinson, newsletter, 2.20.06.
37. Jack Robinson, newsletter, 2.20.06.
38. Jack Robinson, newsletter, 5.3 and 9.18.06.

In 2006, the board of FATEB announced that the current doyen of the school would be leaving at the end of the 2006–2007 academic year. At that point, Dr. Abel Ndjéraréou would have completed seven years of service as doyen. The board promptly began a search for his successor, who would become the fifth doyen to guide this institution in its thirtieth year of developing competent, principled leaders needed in African churches.[39]

Changes in the school continued. In the 2006–2007 school year, with the new primary school buildings completed, enrollment there had climbed to 800 children each day. Half came in the mornings, and the other half studied in the afternoons.[40]

Electrical power shortages had been troubling the campus community for years. This problem arose because turbines at the dam in the national up-river power station had broken down and had not been repaired or replaced. Most evenings were spent by the light of a couple of candles in campus residences. This reduced the time available for productive work in the library. City power was also being cut off during major periods of the daylight hours in unpredictable patterns. When the work of students and staff depended increasingly on computers, printers, copiers, and the internet, trying to work without electricity was a serious interruption. The campus didn't have a diesel generator nor the $20,000 needed to purchase one. This power shortage added yet another challenge to achieving learning goals and administrative functions in an already difficult environment.[41]

2007–2008: NUPANGA WEANZANA APPOINTED DOYEN

In 2007, FATEB announced the appointment of its new doyen, Dr. Nupanga Weanzana. Dr. Nupanga was born near Kinshasa, the capital city of today's Democratic Republic of Congo. His family roots were in northwest Congo near Gemena, where he married Angèle. Nupanga received a scholarship from the Evangelical Free Church to study theology at FATEB in 1985. Following graduation in 1990, Nupanga and Angèle returned to Zaire where Nupanga directed a theological school, pastored a church, and worked in denominational leadership roles. In 1995, Nupanga was invited to return to FATEB as its vice-doyen (executive vice-president) and to teach Old Testament. Four years later, he, his wife and their five children moved

---

39. Jack Robinson, newsletter, 1.2.07.
40. Jack Robinson, newsletter, 10.26.06.
41. Jack Robinson, newsletter, 1.2.07.

to South Africa where he completed a doctorate in Old Testament at the University of Pretoria. In 2003, Dr. Nupanga returned to Bangui where he served as academic dean and professor of Old Testament. Four years later, in July 2007, the board of governors appointed him doyen of FATEB, a responsibility he still carries out as this history is being written eighteen years later in 2025. He has guided the seminary with skill, integrity, wisdom, and grace as it fulfills its mission in Africa.[42]

One of Nupanga's first projects with his faculty and staff in 2007 was to initiate a strategic planning process designed to chart the seminary's course for the next five years. Isaac Zokoué had begun his tenure as doyen in similar fashion. A serious attempt was made to listen carefully to employees, students, financial contributors, and alumni. Small groups evaluated the current state of the seminary and proposed ways that the institution could more effectively serve the churches of Africa. New academic programs were considered, ways of strengthening internships were discussed, and ideas for improving communications with prospective students, graduates, and supporters of the school were noted. The continued importance on prayer and loving relationships within the campus community was evident. Morale was high, and the enthusiasm of the faculty and staff was palpable.[43]

Off-campus, the US embassy in Bangui reopened with a staff of four Americans and an ambassador intent on stimulating economic development in C.A.R. in every way possible. In a context of acute poverty, this prospect was a welcome development. Eleven years earlier, the two hundred serious businesses in the capital had been reduced to just thirty because of civil conflicts. By the end of 2007, the number of businesses had risen again to about 150 and was continuing to grow. The signs of security and civil stability were the most positive seen in over a decade. This situation helped FATEB greatly in the early days of Dr. Nupanga's leadership.[44]

At the beginning of 2008, Dr. Nupanga wrote a brief message to friends and supporters of FATEB in which he described his view of the work that the seminary needed to undertake.

> The fast-growing Church in sub-Saharan Africa constitutes a big challenge for the whole Church. There is an urgent need for well-trained and well-equipped servant-leaders. Unfortunately, many churches cannot afford the full cost for good quality training.

---

42. Jack Robinson, newsletters, 4.17, 7.7, and 9.26.07; Jack Robinson, biographical sketch of Dr. Nupanga Weanzana, 2007.

43. Jack Robinson, newsletter, 12.4.07.

44. Jack Robinson, newsletter, 12.4.07.

An African Dream

As for FATEB specifically, Nupanga went on to write,

> We are facing many challenges this year. Pray for students and professors. Pray for financial provision for scholarships. Pray for continued stability and peace in this country which hosts us.[45]

The quality of the school's faculty was enriched as younger African professors returned to FATEB with excellent training from some of the world's finest graduate schools. Many graduates were carrying out effective ministries in church leadership, in mission outreach and in pastoral training schools in west and central Africa, plus Madagascar, despite their anxiety over violence, widespread insecurity, and a need for greater peace and justice. It was sad to observe the weak economic conditions at FATEB. By early January 2008, the faculty and staff had not yet received their December salaries, and FATEB was carrying significant debt. It was hard to see dedicated faculty and staff working without adequate compensation for themselves and their families. The margin between being able to put food on the table and having hungry children was narrow.[46]

The response to this need on the part of several dozen individuals, two churches, and a foundation over the month of February was extraordinary. Gifts totaling $167,927 were received, an amount equivalent to about one-third of FATEB's annual budget at that time. Most of the funds were designated for faculty support, general operations, including staff salaries, and student scholarships. Salaries through February 2008 were paid, and funds for March were in hand. Government debts for taxes and social security were retired. Financial aid for most current students and some applicants for the new school year was available. Though some residual debt remained, gratitude for these generous friends was deeply felt, and many prayers of thanks were offered to God.[47]

Dr. Nupanga spent three weeks in March 2008 visiting friends of the seminary in the United States. During this visit, Nupanga saw American Christians who expressed the interest and care that they and many other people there have for the churches in Africa. He felt he was among brothers and sisters.[48]

---

45. Nupanga Weanzana, letter to FATEB friends, January 2008.

46. Jack Robinson, newsletter, 2.7.08.

47. Jack Robinson, newsletter, 3.4.08. The Crowell Trust (USA) provided generous and timely financial assistance.

48. Jack Robinson, newsletter, 5.2.08.

FATEB's campus chaplain from Madagascar, Christopher Rabarioelina, also arrived in Chicago in 2008. He and his wife, Marceline, were graduates of FATEB. For many years, she directed the Women's School on the campus while he led the seminary's spiritual life activities. Christopher had recently suffered a detached retina in his right eye. With no retinal surgeons in the Central African Republic, an ophthalmologist there told him he needed outside help as soon as possible to save his eye. At Wheaton Eye Clinic (USA), an ophthalmologist, Dr. Richard Gieser, assured us that the clinic would do the surgery free of charge if Rabarioelina could get to Chicago. He was able to make the trip, was warmly received at the clinic, and had his retina reattached through complicated surgery. Two weeks later, Chaplain Rabarioelina was back at FATEB with 80 percent of his vision restored in his damaged eye. What an encouragement this was, not only to him, but also to his wife and the whole campus community.[49]

On July 31, 2008, twenty men and women from six French-speaking nations graduated with bachelor's and master's degrees, along with the women graduates who were awarded diplomas after three years of studies in the Women's School. The closing ceremonies were attended by several members of the C.A.R. government and representatives from the countries of the graduates. Such occasions were always a cause for ceremony and celebration. After graduation, four of the graduates returned to Angola, Cameroon, Chad, and Senegal, three to the D.R. Congo, and thirteen remained in the Central African Republic, their home country. The security of the Central African graduates was once again an issue because three different rebel groups from nations bordering C.A.R. had spilled into the northeastern and southeastern areas of the country.[50]

2008–2009: HIV/AIDS CONFERENCE CONDUCTED AT FATEB

The new academic year 2008–2009 saw 34 students admitted into the degree programs. After 31 years of equipping people for ministry, FATEB's reputation had been solidly established. For the students, financing remained the biggest obstacle. Many of the applicants accepted for classes were mature men and women who had already demonstrated their gifts for serving Evangelical churches but had not had opportunity for the biblical,

49. Jack Robinson, newsletter, 5.2.08.
50. Jack Robinson, newsletter, 7.30.08.

theological, and missiological studies they needed to maximize their effectiveness as church leaders. They enrolled in FATEB to complete those studies.[51]

By the beginning of August 2008, Dr. Nupanga had served for ten months as doyen of FATEB. Realizing how different his responsibilities were from his years as a professor, he commented on what he thought about serving as doyen: "Teachers are really free people," he said. He explained that professors do not have employees to lead, funds to raise, students to recruit, finances to manage, government offices to satisfy, personnel problems to solve, infrastructure breakdowns to fix, and people on three continents to keep informed of what's going on through travel, electronic communications, updated literature, and speaking engagements. Nupanga was learning that being doyen was a demanding job for anyone who would take the responsibility seriously.[52]

As Dr. Nupanga began his second year as doyen, forty new students enrolled in the degree programs. Nupanga and his colleagues had painfully but successfully reduced the operating expense of the seminary by 17 percent, a percentage that represented $100,000 of their total operating budget.[53]

In addition to the economic management and security challenges that the seminary faced, the HIV/AIDS epidemic continued to complicate life in much of Africa. To help Christians address this situation in C.A.R.'s capital, FATEB held a three-day conference in November 2008 led by Dr. Arthur Ammann, an internationally acclaimed researcher and expert on the virus. He arrived with a team that included an African medical doctor and two experienced African health workers in the field of HIV/AIDS who were serving in Goma, Democratic Republic of Congo. Joined by a Central African doctor, these people made major presentations each morning to 225 local church leaders and senior seminary students who attended the conference. Each afternoon the participants worked in small groups to design strategies for ministry that fit local realities. By the end of the conference, the Bangui Declaration, drafted by Dr. Nupanga on the basis of small group work, was adopted by the participants as a guide for future church ministry to people impacted by the epidemic.[54]

51. Jack Robinson, newsletter, 7.30.08.
52. Jack Robinson, newsletter, 7.30.08.
53. Jack Robinson, newsletter, 12.9.08.
54. Jack Robinson, newsletter, 12.9.08.

A key emphasis in this special HIV/AIDS training for both the campus community and the surrounding churches was the importance of protecting women and children. The participants agreed that the churches should be places of refuge and compassionate care rather than places of judgment. People infected with HIV had often been unjustly condemned, mostly because of fear and ignorance about the disease. Many were literally dying of AIDS in Bangui each day. Among its 700,000 inhabitants, over 70,000 were infected with this deadly virus. The minister of health spoke at the FATEB conference, admitting that the problem was too big for the C.A.R. government. He asked the churches to do all they could to prevent the spread of the virus and to care for those afflicted. A decision was made to prepare a training curriculum that both the seminary and the churches could use to guide Christians in expressing the love and hope that God offers through Christ to suffering individuals and families.[55]

As a follow up to the HIV/AIDS conference, 200 Evangelical churches in Bangui planned, for the coming March 2009, to participate in a week of solidarity with those infected and affected by the epidemic. Education, treatment, and care would accompany a call to carry out the recommendations of the Bangui Declaration earlier approved during the HIV/AIDS conference. The churches had the potential of doing more than any other institution in central Africa to stop the spread of this disease. They were being asked to take informed, compassionate action as part of their commitment to follow Jesus in loving their neighbors as themselves. Motivated FATEB students would be part of this effort.

Graduation took place on June 11, 2009. At such events, it was not just the family, friends, and government representatives of the graduates who celebrated; it was the students as well. A few years earlier, one of the married women who was scheduled to receive her master's degree had gone into labor the morning of graduation day. At 2:00 p.m. she gave birth to her baby. But she wasn't about to miss her other big event. At 4:00 p.m., with a friend in the audience holding her newborn infant, she walked across the assembly hall platform to receive her diploma![56]

---

55. Jack Robinson, newsletter, 12.9.08.
56. Jack Robinson, newsletter, 7.10.09.

An African Dream

2009–2010: DISTANCE EDUCATION PROGRAM IN CHRISTIAN LEADERSHIP

The new academic year 2009–2010 began on September 1 with a faculty retreat and academic council meetings. The board of governors met in September as well. Students were scheduled to be present on October 17 for an opening campus worship service, followed by the beginning of classes on Monday morning, October 19. The academic year ran until July 9, 2010.[57]

FATEB's curricular innovations in support of its mission had included a program for training national Bible translators in partnership with Wycliffe Bible Translators known as SIL. Another addition to the curriculum included a distance education program in Christian leadership in conjunction with Development Associates International called DAI. Furthermore, the doctoral program inaugurated in 2005, designed especially for forming seminary professors, was now functioning. Other innovations by this time reflected the concern of FATEB leaders to serve the local community as it was doing through the three-year preschool, the six-year primary school, as well as the four-year middle school begun in 2009. The diversity of these programs constituted for the students a model of holistic concern for a wide range of human needs. It also increased the appreciation of the C.A.R. government and its Bangui population for the value of this institution. In addition, FATEB's general education programs for children and youth were helping to underwrite the financial expenses of the seminary.[58]

On June 16, 2010, a fire burned up the structure and equipment that distributed electrical current to all the FATEB campus buildings. The diesel generator that provided backup power for the seminary was also damaged. No one was injured, but the fire left the campus without electricity. With six weeks left to the end of the school year, without lights, computers, internet access, or fans in the tropical heat, the school could not function normally. With great flexibility and perseverance, the students and staff found ways to manage until July graduation. By September 2010, repairs had been made. However, generator problems continued until the generator was replaced with a more powerful model several years later.[59]

---

57. Jack Robinson, newsletter, 9.29.09.
58. Jack Robinson, newsletter, 5.6.10.
59. Jack Robinson, newsletters, 6.19.10, 9.8.10.

2010–2011: ANNUAL VISITS TO GRADUATES IN MINISTRY BEGIN A SECOND DECADE

With the beginning of classes in the 2010–2011 school year, 77 students enrolled in the bachelor's and master's degree programs and 22 more in the Women's School diploma program. Eighty students were enrolled in the distance education master's program in Christian leadership offered by DAI, and nearly 1,000 children and young people were coming to campus daily for preschool and general education up through middle school. Students in the degree programs had come from Benin, Burkina Faso, Cameroon, Central African Republic, Chad, D.R. Congo, Republic of Congo, Madagascar, Niger, Rwanda, and Senegal. This level of diversity enriched the network of FATEB students and graduates who were spread over francophone Africa and Madagascar. It also contributed to the unity and strength of the church as students learned to appreciate the distinctives of brother- and sister-Christians from their diverse contexts. This character of the seminary encouraged students to look for ways to support one another.[60]

To evaluate the importance of an educational institution, a look at its faculty, its facilities, and its students provides a significant perspective. However, FATEB's primary mission was not to give its students a great educational experience. Rather, it was to see what the students would do after graduation to strengthen the churches and serve people throughout west and central Africa and Madagascar. In 2011, a series of visits were made to FATEB alumni in their respective fields of service, this time in northeastern D.R. Congo and Uganda. These visits included meeting with nine graduates and their families who were serving with Anglican, Brethren, Baptist, and non-denominational churches. Two were senior pastors, five were professors in Christian universities, one was engaged in Bible translation, and one had become the archbishop of the Anglican Church of the D.R. Congo. Among the wives of these men, one was directing a women's school, several were training women in their churches, two were ministering to abused women, one was working with widows and orphans, and one was involved in medical work as a nurse. All the women were mothers.

Especially striking was not just the leadership these men and women were providing for their churches and institutions in the region, but that they had served in this way through many of the previous 15 years of war in

---

60. Jack Robinson, newsletter, 12.4.10.

both Congos and Uganda that had involved traumatic losses and atrocities, taking the lives of some of their own family members and friends. Homes had been pillaged, properties had been lost, and some of these graduates had had to flee to the forest for safety or to other cities to wait out the violence. In 2002, a community at the Nyankunde Medical Center, an hour's drive from an Evangelical seminary in Bunia, northeastern Congo, had suffered the massacre of over 1,000 of its villagers. The seminary graduates who lived through this violence had to cope with their own trauma as well as to try to help those around them. Yet, these families described experiences of God's faithfulness. Their faith and hope and their spirit of reconciliation and positive vision for the future were very evident.

When questioned about how their seminary training at FATEB had been most helpful to them, graduates often spoke of the relationships they had forged with students from other African countries and church traditions that gave them a sense of solidarity with a large company of unseen companions with whom they were serving together in Africa. The FATEB faculty had also helped them to become independent learners. In addition, the Women's School had trained and equipped the wives of these men. Together, they served the Lord. These encounters with graduates scattered throughout French-speaking Africa convinced us that the work of FATEB was indeed worth what so many people both inside and out of Africa were investing in it.[61]

On July 30, 2011, 30 students composed FATEB's twenty-ninth graduating class. At this time, some of the alumni from the first graduating class of 1982 were approaching retirement. For almost three decades, their lives had been used to strengthen churches and enrich society. Over 700 pastors and church leaders for the francophone church in Africa had been equipped by FATEB since African Christians founded this seminary in 1977.[62]

2011-2012: CONSTRUCTING A CONFERENCE CENTER FOR CONTINUING EDUCATION

During the latter part of 2011, the administration in Bangui discussed the possibility of going beyond the training of formal church leaders to address additional educational needs of the Christian and general population. An English language institute was proposed. A center for teacher training

61. Jack Robinson, newsletter, May 2011.
62. Jack Robinson, newsletters, 7.29.11 and 10.26.11.

in general education reflecting Christian values was another proposal. A practical business development program focused on entrepreneurship and economic development was a third proposal. Small pilot programs were tried in each of these three areas. Had they continued to show promise, they might have become the core of a Christian university. However, FATEB leaders felt that the primary mission of the institution should not be compromised by the addition of other disciplines into the seminary curriculum. If such programs were to be developed into degree-granting programs, it was felt they should be offered in the framework of a separate institution, such as a Christian university.[63]

Despite the reticence of FATEB leadership to convert the seminary into a Christian university, the possibility of offering practical non-formal learning programs to Christians remained an attractive option. Continuing education was clearly of interest to female students in the Women's School who wished to acquire professional skills that would enable them and their families to benefit economically and would give them specialized means for helping others. Practical courses in computer skills, expertise in sewing, entrepreneurship, financial management, disease prevention and health promotion were highly valued by these women. Seminars, workshops, and conferences for church leaders, both male as well as female, could address other current needs of Christians who were not enrolled in formal educational programs.

To facilitate the development of such non-formal learning programs, a decision was made to construct a conference center building on FATEB's campus. This center would offer continuing education and the improvement of ministry skills through its conferences, workshops, and non-formal programs. Guest rooms for people coming to campus and conference rooms for participants would be included in the building. Planning had progressed over several months, and proposals were communicated to some of FATEB's foreign partner organizations. Several organizations in Europe and North America promised funds for such a center, and construction was intended to begin in 2012.[64]

As the ministry of the seminary continued to grow for adult learners, a surprising increase was taking place in the programs of general education for the children and youth. Over the previous few years, FATEB had

---

63. Jack Robinson, newsletters, 7.29.11 and 10.26.11.

64. Jack Robinson, newsletter, 2.23.12. The Cornerstone Trust (Grand Rapids) provided essential project support.

already come to manage a preschool, kindergarten, elementary, and middle school. Beginning in 2012, a three-year secondary school, called a *lycée* in the French educational tradition, was added. Each of these schools had begun in response to students in the degree programs who wanted a reliable education for their children while at FATEB. But the rapid expansion was the result of people off campus in the city who also wanted their children educated at FATEB. The modest fees they paid for their children and young people to come weekdays for classes was also helping to stabilize FATEB's financial condition.[65]

By mid-year 2012, the new conference center was under construction, supervised by Gaston Kingue from Cameroon. It was designed for two dozen double guest rooms, a kitchen, dining room, and meeting areas. In addition to facilitating continuing education programs, the center would receive visitors and work teams from abroad who could assist the school in various ways. Eighty percent of the financing was in hand, and the project generated wide interest within the campus community.[66]

2012–2013: COUP D'ÉTAT SENDS MANY FATEB STUDENTS TO CAMEROON CAMPUS

In October 2012, new students from twelve different countries arrived. Five west African countries and seven central African countries were represented in the ninety-four students enrolled in the residential programs. Eleven doctoral students also began studies that year. A new professor of Old Testament, Dr. Mavinga from the D.R. Congo, joined the faculty with his wife, Charlotte, who taught in the Women's School. FATEB's pastoral theology professor and the school librarian began doctoral studies, and two new staff members were hired to replace them.[67]

In November 2012, warning signs of trouble around the perimeter of the Central African Republic were appearing as terrorist and rebel attacks from groups in bordering countries like Chad, South Sudan, and Uganda came into C.A.R., wreaking havoc on local populations. The government of C.A.R. did not have adequate military personnel to prevent these hostilities in many of the border areas of the country that is slightly

---

65. Jack Robinson, newsletter, 2.23.12.
66. Jack Robinson, newsletter, 7.20.12.
67. Jack Robinson, newsletters, 10.4 and 11.28.12.

larger geographically than France but with a population of only five million people.⁶⁸

By December 2012, the security situation in C.A.R. had become unstable. The American embassy in Bangui closed and evacuated its American employees. Most of the expatriate missionaries left the country. Rebels stopped their advance just a few miles northeast of Bangui and insisted on talks with the government. After a week of negotiations, a power-sharing deal led to the signing of a peace agreement.⁶⁹

Sadly, the peace agreement held for only a few weeks. A coup d'état took place on March 24, 2013, in which 5,000 fighters seized power from the Bozizé government in a military offensive. The president fled from the country, and a tragic week of violence and looting followed. For several days the capital was without city water or electricity. A rebel leader proclaimed himself president of the country, suspended the constitution, and dismissed the country's legislative body. Widespread destruction of the city's infrastructure and businesses left the capital in a precarious state.

The seminary escaped the violence of military and civilian looters. Students and staff patrolled the campus all night long during the last week of March 2013 to discourage bandits from entering the property. Daily prayer meetings brought the campus community together with a deepened sense of its dependence on God. The 300 people living on campus showed amazing resilience, and even some classes were held despite the frightening conditions outside the campus walls.⁷⁰

A humanitarian crisis was growing in C.A.R. with a quarter of the population uprooted. People were afraid to plant their fields, starvation was threatening many civilians, and violence and insecurity were driving people out of the country. Foreigners could no longer safely enter it. Though FATEB was in danger, the campus itself was spared violence. United Nations peacekeeping soldiers from nearby countries were housed on campus and guarded FATEB against looters. Hundreds of internally displaced people took refuge on the campus, initially sleeping in classrooms and offices or on the ground. Trying to carry on academic programs in an environment of such upheaval was a tremendous challenge. The rule of law and a semblance of democracy in C.A.R. seemed only memories at this time. Religious tensions increased between the new Muslim government

68. Jack Robinson, newsletters, 10.4 and 11.28.12.
69. Jack Robinson, newsletter, 2.5.13.
70. Jack Robinson, newsletter, 3.30.13.

and the majority Christian population. Nevertheless, students and teachers alike worked diligently and courageously to complete their classes by the end of the school year.[71]

In April 2013, Dr. Nupanga called together several key people in Yaoundé, the capital city of neighboring Cameroon, to discuss the future of FATEB. Recommendations made by Dr. Nupanga to make the degree programs accessible to students in Yaoundé, Cameroon, as well as in Bangui, were carried out. If FATEB were to continue to pursue its mission of serving all French-speaking Africa, offering the master's and doctoral programs in Cameroon would be essential for students from outside C.A.R. to be able to study in a context of security. With military protection for FATEB in C.A.R., the academic programs there were able to continue serving Central African students. The two weeks of classes lost to the hostilities extended the school year into August 2013. By late June of that year, three-fourths of C.A.R. had been without medical care since the March 24 coup, and many families had fled into the forests where there was no food. At the same time, church leaders in Bangui were gathering with congregational members to look for ways to bring peace, justice, and redemption to their country.[72]

On August 3, 2013, despite catastrophic conditions in C.A.R., FATEB held its thirty-second annual graduation ceremony. More than 1,000 people overflowed the campus assembly hall to celebrate the graduates, 47 of them in all. To 23 master's graduates and 11 bachelor's graduates, degrees were awarded in biblical, theological, and missiological studies. Another twelve master's degrees in organizational leadership were awarded, along with one doctoral degree. Outside of areas in the city guarded by peacekeepers, the humanitarian crisis continued, as reported on August 7, 2013, in a *New York Times* front page article.[73] C.A.R. was experiencing an ongoing, inhumane, and heart-breaking tragedy, unknown to most of the world but understood by graduates preparing to leave the relative safety of FATEB's campus.[74]

---

71. Jack Robinson, newsletter, 5.1.13.
72. Jack Robinson, newsletter, 6.25.13.
73. Nossiter, "Violent and Chaotic."
74. Jack Robinson, newsletter, 8.8.13.

2013–2014: INTERNALLY DISPLACED PEOPLE FLEE TO FATEB'S CAMPUS IN BANGUI

Classes for the 2013–2014 school year began in early October, though with reduced numbers of students. During daylight hours, students and staff were able to leave campus to purchase food and other necessities for daily life. People from the interior areas of the country continued to seek refuge in surrounding countries as more foreign soldiers entered C.A.R. to live off the local population by extortion.

By October 2013, a second campus site for the educational programs of FATEB was established in Yaoundé, Cameroon. SIL-Wycliffe, FATEB's long term partners in training national Bible translators, was especially helpful in making their facilities in Yaoundé accessible to FATEB. There, doctoral students of FATEB planned to gather for classes in November and December 2013. Classes for master's students were planned for January 2014. Office and classroom space to rent was identified, and initially, faculty would travel between Bangui and Yaoundé to maintain academic programs at both sites. Jean Patrick N'Kolo Fanga became academic secretary for the Yaoundé campus. Two other cities in French-speaking Africa, Kinshasa in D.R. Congo and Ouagadougou in Burkina Faso, were also being explored as possible sites for branch campuses, considering the insecurity of the Central African Republic.[75]

As Christmas 2013 approached, it was easy to wonder what had happened to the angels' message of "Peace on earth, Good will toward men." The political conflict in C.A.R. of the preceding decade was taking on a religious dimension. Both Christians and Muslims were resorting to the ancient practice of using religion as a political tool. Churches and mosques were being burned, people identified as Christians and Muslims were killing one another while hate and revenge were tearing the country apart as political elements struggled and fought for power. Central Africans were suffering terribly.

With FATEB students from countries other than C.A.R. leaving Bangui due to the hostilities, the creation of a second campus on the Yaoundé site was necessary for FATEB to maintain its regional mission to all of francophone Africa. Keeping the seminary economically viable looked difficult. But having a place where students from other parts of French-speaking Africa could study in safety gave hope for the future of FATEB. And the

---

75. Jack Robinson, newsletter, 10.29.13.

celebration of Christmas reminded everyone of God's protection over the past traumatic year they had lived through and of the promise of his ongoing presence and persistent love for them all.[76]

The years 2013 and 2014 were among the most turbulent years of outside disturbances that the FATEB community had ever experienced. The disruptions to the master's level students were the most serious because many of them were not Central Africans. They had come to study from other African countries. Their studies had been interrupted by the tragic events in C.A.R. in 2013. By February 2014, many of the student families were moving to Cameroon, hoping to complete their master's work there and to graduate in mid-year.

Further complicating life on the Bangui campus was the presence of internally displaced persons who had fled their homes in dangerous areas of the capital. About 1,500 such refugees sought shelter and security at FATEB to escape violence in the city. The FATEB administration made a conscious decision to permit this influx of terrified people, realizing that the campus was a haven because it was located across the street from C.A.R.'s telecommunications center, which was being heavily guarded by French troops.

In January 2014, the self-proclaimed rebel president was forced out of office. He had been incapable of stopping the looting, killing, insecurity, and chaos. A woman who had been serving as mayor of Bangui was made the provisional president of the country. She called upon "her children" on both sides of the conflict to stop killing one another. Her pleas seemed to fall on deaf ears.

The main rebel group, known as Seleka, was primarily driven by greed for resources and showed little regard for the good of the country. Following the March 24, 2013, coup, the population had suffered more than eight months of looting, raping, and killing by the Seleka rebels. Muslims constituted a minority group in the predominantly Christian C.A.R. This fact encouraged some of the rebels to make religious conflict an excuse for their attacks. But in December 2013, anti-Seleka forces, drawn mainly from those who identified as Christian, killed several senior Seleka officers, prompting a revengeful response of indiscriminate killing in Bangui neighborhoods. Over 100,000 terrified Bangui residents fled their homes to camp at the international airport that was guarded by French troops. Tragically, angry mobs interpreted the wave of slaughter as Muslims trying

---

76. Jack Robinson, newsletter, 12.24.13.

to exterminate Christians. Non-Muslims responded with genocidal attacks on Muslims who then began fleeing the country.[77]

Surrounded by physical danger, FATEB had become not only a place of refuge for internally displaced families and individuals but also a place of prayer. People who had never worshiped or prayed together gathered with the campus community, encouraging one another, praying for peace, and planning joint action in support of non-violence and forgiveness. Bonds of mutual concern and solidarity were forged across lines of ethnic and denominational differences to create a profound sense of community. People were expressing their desire to follow Jesus and his call to love one's enemies rather than to seek revenge.

At this time of insecurity outside the campus, internally the founding generation of FATEB was beginning to pass away. On January 1, 2014, Dr. Paul White, the first doyen of the seminary, died almost 37 years after he had opened the doors to the first students in 1977. Dr. Isaac Zokoué, who negotiated the first land grant for the school and served from 1986 to the year 2000 as its doyen, was suffering a life-threatening illness. He would live only a few more months. Pastor Philippe Doukofiona, an early graduate and long-term administrator at FATEB, was also experiencing a serious illness. These men of the pioneer generation had laid the foundations and built upon them much of what the school had eventually become. A younger group of men and women would need to carry on the mission of FATEB to strengthen the churches of central and west francophone Africa through training leaders who could communicate the teaching of the Scriptures, embody the character of Jesus, and understand the times in which they lived.[78]

On March 3, 2014, master's classes reconvened in Yaoundé, Cameroon. A couple from Michigan, USA, John and Marilyn Roughley, with the help of other volunteers, spent several weeks in Yaoundé overseeing the equipping of classrooms and offices as well as spaces for a computer lab and library. Because traveling outside the capital by road risked attacks by rebels, about 50 students flew from C.A.R. to Cameroon to complete their studies, either in their final (third) year of the bachelor's program or in the two-year master's program.

By April 2014, violence in Bangui was less continuous, but almost 1,000 displaced people were still living in tents on FATEB's campus. Some

77. Jack Robinson, newsletter, 2.8.14.
78. Jack Robinson, newsletter, 2.8.14.

families went to their homes in the city during the day but needed the protection of the campus at night. Despite insecurity in the city, the kindergarten, primary, and secondary schools reopened in early 2014, as did the Women's School and the first two years of the bachelor's program. In addition to the branch campus in Cameroon, the administration was still considering the possibility of additional sites in countries where they had received invitations: D.R. Congo, Senegal, and Burkina Faso.[79]

2014–2015: AFTER 41 YEARS OF SERVICE TO FATEB, ISAAC ZOKOUÉ DIES

On September 12, 2014, Dr. Isaac Zokoué passed away in Bangui. Zokoué had done more than any other person to shape FATEB over the 41 years that had passed since its conception. Besides negotiating for the land on which FATEB stands, he provided board leadership for the school in its early years. He then served as doyen of the seminary for 14 years. After stepping down from his chief executive officer role in 2000, he led the project to create a doctoral program for the school and directed it until his death.

Four thousand people, including the C.A.R. prime minister and fifteen other government ministers, attended his funeral on FATEB's campus. He had been not only a theologian and educator but also a pastor in the capital city and a national peacemaker, leading national reconciliation conferences and dialogues for the entire country. Zokoué was selected for these roles because of his reputation for integrity and justice. One of his Dutch colleagues at FATEB wrote, "I will never forget the picture of him, on his knees on the stairs of the Parliament building, washing the feet of those leaders who had been of opposing parties, after an aborted coup d'état, and violent clashes in which many people died, and much was destroyed."

Unusually tall, quiet, thoughtful, and articulate, Zokoué cared deeply for his students, his staff, their families, and his fellow citizens. He was 70 years old when he died and left behind not only his family but also hundreds of graduates of FATEB serving throughout west and central Africa who had been influenced by his teaching and his life. For over several decades, church leaders found in Isaac Zokoué a model of African Christian

---

79. Jack Robinson, newsletter, 4.17.14.

leadership worthy of following, just as he faithfully followed Christ for those many years.[80]

Academic programs in Bangui were completed in late August of 2014. Graduation ceremonies in Cameroon took place in late September for the students from many African countries who had completed bachelor's and master's programs. The interruptions of the academic year had been overcome and the school year completed. The legacy of Dr. Zokoué remained. Nevertheless, the seminary community looked forward to the continuation of its mission of equipping people for ministry, a responsibility that would require collaboration and courage in the context of the armed conflicts still present, the new health challenge of the Ebola virus, and the ongoing pressure of economic hardship for so many Africans.[81]

The year 2015 could be called a year of healing for the FATEB community, though healing beyond the walls of the seminary proceeded more slowly. Several hundred displaced people remained on the campus following two years of trauma, with its threats, destruction, and loss of life. Humanitarian agencies had dug latrines on campus, provided food, erected large tents, and given people sleeping mats and mosquito nets. Ten large families could share the open interior of each tent. There, Muslim and Christian families found shelter together under a common tent roof.[82]

Outside the city, schools were not operating, hospitals destroyed by the rebels had not reopened, and lawlessness reigned throughout the interior of the country. Religion had been used as a tool for political power struggles. The youth of the country, who composed 50 percent of the population, had been seduced into serving the purposes of rebel leaders and then were abandoned when they were no longer needed.[83]

On campus, the large assembly hall became a city meeting place for prayer, for seminars, for discussions, and for planning ways of dealing with the crisis. Government officials, United Nations agencies, relief agencies such as the Red Cross, World Vision, and TEAR Fund, and church groups used FATEB's facilities to talk together about how to bring peace and reconciliation to this troubled country. As the capital became more stable, the schools on campus from preschool to university level programs grew in student numbers beyond pre-crisis levels. At the same time, the depressive

80. Jack Robinson, newsletter, 9.25.14.
81. Jack Robinson, newsletter, 9.25.14.
82. Jack Robinson, newsletter, 2.16.15.
83. Jack Robinson, newsletter, 11.11.14.

impact of the fighting, destruction of businesses, and loss of jobs decreased the ability of churches and families to support those studying in the seminary programs. FATEB had not just survived these two years of turmoil but had exerted positive leadership and service through it.[84]

In January 2015, when African friends and colleagues at FATEB were asked how they had managed over the previous two years of fear and privation, most of them replied, "We were well, by the grace of God." The trauma they had experienced not only drew the students and staff closer together, but it also drew them closer to God. They evidenced strong faith and resolve, even though they knew they might be tested again.[85]

Dr. Nupanga, the doyen, was now responsible for the oversight of two campuses. Graduations on both the Cameroon and Central African Republic campuses were held in July 2015. The graduation events observed by students, staff, and friends of FATEB were not only celebrated because of the success of the students but also because additional men, women, and families were being launched into ministry in several countries of central and west Africa, to serve the Lord, the church, and society.[86]

2015–2016: FATEB'S SCHOOLS FOR YOUTH KEEP GROWING

In late November 2015, Pope Francis carried out his wish to visit two of the neediest countries of Africa. He chose to go to Uganda and to the Central African Republic. Because of a brief upswing of violence in Bangui just before his visit, there was uncertainty about whether he would come.

Pope Francis did arrive in Bangui on a peace initiative, making a two-day visit to address Catholic, Protestant, and Muslim audiences. He called people to arm themselves with peace, justice, forgiveness, and love instead of the weapons of war. In this suffering, danger-filled country, exerting his moral influence encouraged people to reevaluate their use of violence to reach political and social goals.

In his address to Protestants, given in the multipurpose hall on the FATEB campus, Pope Francis said, "For all too long, your people have experienced troubles and violence, resulting in great suffering. This makes the proclamation of the Gospel even more necessary and urgent. In these

84. Jack Robinson, newsletter, 1.16.15.
85. Jack Robinson, newsletter, 3.31.15.
86. Jack Robinson, newsletter, 7.8.15.

difficult circumstances, the Lord keeps asking us to demonstrate to everyone his tenderness, compassion, and mercy."[87]

The visit of Pope Francis contributed significantly to the reduction of hostilities by the general population toward Muslims. Before his death, Isaac Zokoué had communicated with the president of the Evangelical Association of Churches, the Catholic archbishop, and the leading Muslim imam in C.A.R. about how best to create a platform-for-peace initiative. All three leaders sent strong messages to their constituencies, affirming that the tragic conflict in C.A.R. was not about religion but was rather a political conflict. As people understood this, inter-ethnic and inter-religious tensions in the capital began to subside.[88] At the request of the C.A.R. government, Zokoué had twice before provided leadership in national reconciliation conferences, in 1998 and 2003.

In April 2016, after a year under rebel rule and two years under a transitional government, a new president was elected, Faustin Archange Touadéra. His first goal was to reunite the country. Creating jobs was also a crucial priority. After the displacement of at least a million people, the humanitarian crisis remained, and infrastructure of every sort needed rebuilding. With their campus schools operating, the educational services offered by FATEB at every academic level continued to be in great demand. In contrast to many other local institutions, FATEB was spared looting, destruction, and loss of life.[89]

During the 2015–2016 academic year, over 2,000 children and youth attended FATEB schools. The bachelor of theology program at the Bangui campus grew in its enrollment, and the construction of the two-story Leadership Conference Center moved ahead rapidly once again. In 2016, graduation ceremonies took place in both Bangui and Yaoundé. The academic achievement of the youth in FATEB's secondary school, as measured on the standard achievement test, was at the highest level of all the schools in the capital. The Christian character of the education provided for children and youth on campus represented the formative stages of Christian leadership development that teachers and administrators hoped would strengthen churches and mark Central African society.[90]

---

87. Jack Robinson, newsletter, 12.1.15.
88. Jack Robinson, newsletter, 2.5.16.
89. Jack Robinson, newsletter, 5.3.16.
90. Jack Robinson, newsletter, 8.19.16.

An African Dream

2016–2017: C.A.R. PRESIDENT TOUADÉRA SPEAKS AT FATEB'S FORTIETH ANNIVERSARY

Although master's and doctoral programs were conducted on the Cameroon campus, and a bachelor's program existed there also, several educational programs were available in Bangui. The three-year bachelor of theology degree program and the two-year DAI master of organizational leadership program continued at the Bangui campus, as did the three-year diploma programs of the Women's School. The general education curriculum for children was also operative in Bangui and included a three-year preschool, a six-year primary school, a four-year middle school, and a three-year high school, the *lycée*. These programs of general education in FATEB's schools had evolved step by step over several decades, initially in response to the needs of seminary students' children, and later as a service to the children of parents in the churches of Bangui.

Preparations were made to celebrate the 40-year anniversary of FATEB's institutional life in January 2017. A three-day academic conference preceded a day and a half of special thanksgiving events.[91] The theme of the conference addressed the role of the church in African countries currently experiencing, or recovering from, violent conflict. For the final days of celebration, the general secretary of the Association of Evangelicals in Africa (AEA) joined the event to celebrate God's faithfulness. His presence was fitting since AEA had voted 44 years earlier, in 1973, to create FATEB and its sister English-speaking graduate school in Nairobi.

On the final day of the conference in January 2017, FATEB welcomed C.A.R.'s chief of state, President Touadéra, who arrived with his prime minister, some of his cabinet members, and other government officials. After knighting several FATEB-related individuals, the president made informal remarks to the several hundred people in attendance. He paid special tribute to FATEB for sheltering several thousand internally displaced people over the previous four years. He also thanked FATEB for the many children and youth FATEB had educated in its Christian general education schools, reputed to be among the best in the capital. By this time, enrollment in these schools had reached 2,400 pupils who came to the campus daily to study.

The visits of FATEB friends from other countries helped faculty and staff to realize they had not been forgotten during the preceding four years

---

91. Jack Robinson, newsletter, 11.16.16.

of conflict. People were celebrating the hopeful beginning of a new era of growing peace and stability. The last of the internally displaced people left the campus in that month of January 2017. An American team from Mtelo Ministries (USA) had arrived to work for two months, upgrading some of the older buildings of FATEB. In addition, three new construction projects on campus had been started. The African founders of FATEB in the 1970s had had no idea that this project would be as successful as it had become. Its board of governors and administration gave witness in 2017 to the providence and faithfulness of God that had protected and blessed the institution over the 40 years since it had begun classes in 1977.[92]

In July 2017, FATEB held graduation ceremonies in both Bangui, C.A.R., and Yaoundé, Cameroon. In countries with desperately poor populations, education was the vehicle that enabled young people to move from their traditional backgrounds and into the world of the present and the future. At FATEB, youth and young adults received the knowledge and tools they needed not only to support themselves but also to encourage and lift others with employment skills, improved health, personal development, and spiritual life. General education brought hope to families and communities, and Christian education taught and modeled values that reflected the character of Jesus Christ and brought transformation to individuals and society.[93]

2017–2018: THE WOMEN'S SCHOOL OPENS TO WOMEN FROM BANGUI CHURCHES

One of the benefits of the doctoral studies program at FATEB is that it could help to meet the need for qualified resident professors on its own faculty. This possibility became a reality. Dr. William Mbuluku from the D.R. Congo graduated from FATEB's master's program in 2001, then a master's in New Testament in 2012. He served as head librarian of the seminary for 12 years before enrolling in the doctoral program and completing his work in 2017. Dr. Mbuluku then joined the faculty in Yaoundé to teach New Testament, wanting to lead his students into understanding and faithfully interpreting the New Testament as they carried out their ministries in African churches and society.

---

92. Jack Robinson, newsletter, 2.3.17.
93. Jack Robinson, newsletter, 9.11.17.

Dr. Williams Moloby came from the Republic of Congo and had served as a pastor and Bible school director there. After graduating from FATEB with his master's degree, he served as academic secretary and taught in the seminary for several years. He then enrolled in the FATEB doctoral program and focused his research on the mission of the church in C.A.R., in Chad, and in both Congos. After receiving his doctorate, he joined the FATEB faculty to serve in the Missiology Department of FATEB. Moloby's aim was to inspire his students to assist the African church to become a truly missionary church that would bring spiritual and social transformation to individual lives and communities through the good news of Christ.

Progress on the construction of the Leadership Conference Center on Bangui's campus, which had to be abandoned in 2013, was nearing completion in 2018. In addition, a new generator was purchased, capable of providing electrical power for the entire campus. Internet access was upgraded for students, faculty, and staff. A solar power project was also launched to take advantage of the Central African sun that constitutes a huge energy source. Enrollment of children and youth in FATEB's campus schools kept growing in early 2018, reaching almost 3,000 children and youth who were involved daily in school activities on campus.[94]

Violence erupted once again in Bangui on May 2, 2018, in response to an effort in April 2018 to disarm militants in the capital city. Gunmen with grenades attacked a Roman Catholic church in Bangui, killing 15 people and injuring dozens. Attempts to turn this event into a religious conflict between Muslims and Christians inflamed people on both sides. A few weeks earlier, 28 people had been killed through violent clashes in retaliation against disarmament operations by the United Nations peacekeepers and local security forces. Trying to conduct classes during such insecurity was no easy task.

Despite renewed conflict, the seminary's educational work continued. The Women's School was expanded that year from its service only to student wives to training women from various churches within the city also. The Women's School programs in Christian education, family health management, and skills for generating income were a great encouragement to women, both young and old, who were often responsible for their family's economic survival.

In addition to the PhD doctoral program in Yaoundé, a doctor of ministries program was launched on the Bangui campus in early 2018. For

---

94. Jack Robinson, newsletter, March 2018.

church leaders already in ministry and who had completed their master's level studies, this program offered a chance to strengthen their knowledge and skills for the work to which they were committed. This innovation marked a step forward in FATEB's training not only for those wanting to be equipped for church-related ministries but also a continuing education option for those already engaged in ministry. That year, 21 students enrolled in the new program.[95]

July 2018 marked the end of five years of educational programs on FATEB's second campus in Yaoundé, Cameroon. Graduation was held before an overflow crowd. Degrees awarded included two doctorates, one in theology and one in New Testament; nine master's degrees in several disciplines: biblical studies, theology, missiology, and leadership; four bachelor's degrees in theology; plus a diploma in preaching. Most of these graduates in Cameroon came from countries outside of C.A.R. in west and central Africa.

In Bangui, a high percentage of the students were citizens of the Central African Republic. It was therefore understandable that 1,600 people came to the Bangui graduation ceremony on July 28, 2018. One doctoral degree, four master's degrees in Christian leadership, thirteen bachelor's degrees in theology, and four diplomas to graduates of the Women's School were awarded.[96]

2018–2019: KEY PEOPLE JOIN FATEB'S ADMINISTRATIVE STAFF

In 2018, three key staff positions were filled with outstanding people. To head the administration, Andre Fegouto was appointed. Fegouto, a FATEB graduate, had served several years as president of his denomination, the Eglise Evangélique Baptiste, in western Central African Republic. To direct financial affairs, Marie-Angele Kosseke joined the staff. She is a gifted woman who had been responsible for finance and administration at FATEB's Cameroon campus. The position of general manager was filled by Dr. Paul Mpindi, a FATEB graduate, author, professor, and experienced administrator of pastoral training projects in several French African countries. This team brought strength, vigor, and much needed assistance to FATEB and to its doyen.

95. Jack Robinson, newsletter, May 2018.
96. Jack Robinson, newsletter, 8.27.18.

The Cameroon campus library received a grant of 1,700 books in 2018, written by scholars of New Testament and Christian ethics. The books were given in memory of Dr. Alan F. Johnson, professor for 40 years in the Department of Biblical and Theological Studies of Wheaton College (USA). This special collection of books for research, writing, and teaching gave faculty and students in the master's and doctoral programs in Yaoundé bibliographic resources that Dr. Johnson had assembled throughout his teaching career.[97]

In February 2019, 14 rebel groups in C.A.R. signed a peace accord with the Central African government. After six years of military conflicts, rape, material destruction, refugee terror, revenge killings, and ongoing human crisis, this development was positive news. Almost a quarter of the country's civilian population had fled their homes, seeking shelter and safety either within other regions of the country or beyond its borders. UNICEF called C.A.R. the most dangerous place in the world to be a child. Two of every three children there needed humanitarian aid.

By 2019, the growing FATEB schools for children and youth represented a large part of its educational work. While school fees helped to defray the costs of operating the degree programs, it didn't seem right to the seminary leaders to regard these schools simply as additional sources of financial support. They represented another important way of helping FATEB fulfill its mission of equipping people for roles of Christian leadership in the churches and societies of French-speaking Africa. Thus, a decision was made to embrace the education of these children and youth as an integral part of FATEB's mission and commitment to Christian education. FATEB leaders wanted these young people to study in a community where Christian values were lived as well as taught and then leave school permanently marked by their Christian education.

A brief profile of two Central African students in the Bangui degree programs offers a glimpse of their development at the university level. Aubin, the eventual president of the student body, enrolled in FATEB because he believed that biblical and theological studies would be essential for his future ministry. He said, "The needs in the churches and in society are enormous. I plan to begin work in the church, teaching the Word of God with the conviction that the Good News of Jesus is holistic, touching all of human life." Aubin said he also wanted to create radio and television broadcasts that would help citizens of his country flourish in every area of life.

97. Jack Robinson, newsletter, 12.11.18.

Broadening the Vision—Ndjéraréou and Weanzana

Viviane, while a FATEB student, was already engaged in work with female soldiers in the national army. She said, "I want to contribute to the moral and spiritual well-being of the feminine military, a role usually given to male chaplains." She continued, "I want to work in my local community in the education of children and the preparation of young women for marriage. I also look forward to a pastoral ministry with women, especially touching their marriages and their marital relationships."[98]

To accomplish its mission, FATEB needed physical space in which to conduct its work. The 12-acre campus in Bangui was an extraordinary gift, but it needed infrastructure systems for electricity, water, sewer, and internet access to meet the needs of several thousand students on its campus daily. Beginning in 2006, competent men and women from an American organization called Mtelo Ministries volunteered for weeks at a time to strengthen the physical systems of the seminary. The Martins, Roughleys, and Bergs invested deeply in improving the campus infrastructure and its administration. To extend evening hours for work, solar panels were installed to collect energy during the day that was converted to electricity at night to illuminate the library for the students wishing to study there. In the past, well water was pumped into the campus water tower, using city electricity. With a solar pump, the tower could be kept full without using city power. Corroded and partially plugged pipes have been replaced, faucets fixed, and outside spigots capped. A kitchen for the new building begun in 2012 needed equipment: refrigerators, a microwave oven, a freezer, and cabinets for dishes and supplies. Meeting these needs that enabled the campus buildings and programs to function efficiently were what these generous friends made possible.[99]

In July 2019, 26 men and women became part of FATEB's thirty-seventh graduating class from the two campuses. Afterward, they returned to churches in a variety of Protestant denominations in central and west Africa to serve their congregations and society. The peace agreement signed in Bangui in February 2019 had followed six years of civil war and was now enabling the educational programs of the seminary to be completed without disruption. The United Nations reported a decrease in the number of reported human rights violations since the signature of the February 2019 agreement, though security was still difficult to maintain, especially in the interior of C.A.R. While the Cameroon campus remained calm, the

---

98. Jack Robinson, newsletter, 3.8.19.
99. Jack Robinson, newsletter, 5.22.19.

presence of peacekeeping troops in Bangui was essential to maintaining the stability needed for the seminary to function well.[100]

2019–2020: NEW LEADERSHIP CONFERENCE CENTER

Although the primary motivation for the creation of FATEB was to provide university level training for church leaders in francophone Africa, FATEB's founders insisted on launching the Women's School that began in 1977 when classes in the degree program commenced. In French, the official name of the Women's School translates as "School for Biblical Study and the Advancement of Women." An African member of the administration explained the importance of the Women's School in this way:

> With extreme poverty destroying much of the continent, African mothers have become both the economic and emotional pillars that carry the weight of this beleaguered continent. What makes things worse is the fact that 60% of Sub-Saharan African women are illiterate. Although many young girls do attend schools, very few of them have access to higher education. This is especially true for the wives of future pastors who attend the seminary in Bangui.[101]

Though some women were doing outstanding work in FATEB's master's and doctoral programs, many were still coming from remote towns and villages, barely able to read or write. Thus, for many women, education at FATEB began with French literacy classes. Then, the three-year women's training program assisted them to study the Bible and develop practical skills that included reading, writing, sewing, clothes manufacture, nutritional cooking, family management, computer training, and Christian leadership. In 2019, 39 female students were welcomed to the Women's School from C.A.R., Cameroon, Mali, and from churches in Bangui.

Marceline Rabarioelina, from Madagascar, who thrived as a student in the three-year Woman's School program, became its director. For several decades she has brought competent, practical teaching to student wives in the Women's School while modeling mature Christian character through her ministry there. In our visits with alumni throughout francophone Africa, graduates of the Women's School impressed us with their ability to

---

100. Jack Robinson, newsletter, 8.12.19.
101. Jack Robinson, newsletter, 11.20.19.

transmit knowledge and skills to those around them who lacked this kind of education. The way they exhibited Christian values and relationships with their husbands and children were instructive models for members of their churches.

FATEB inaugurated a new campus structure in February 2020. Called the Leadership Conference Center, work on this building had begun in 2012. However, construction stopped in 2013 when rebels entered the capital of Bangui. For the next four years, hostilities prevented additional work on the center. In 2017, construction recommenced. Finally functional in 2020, the center received its first visitors who had come for an international conference on health, illness, and healing. Local health professionals joined the 250 conference participants that included 35 international visitors from Europe, North America, and other African countries. When African Christians became ill, many went to their pastor for prayer, to a medical doctor for prescriptions, and sometimes to a traditional healer for other remedies. What light did the Bible shed on these issues? How could Christians understand health challenges in ways that reflected God's love and enabled them to serve the ill compassionately and effectively? With the Leadership Conference Center, FATEB was able to facilitate discussions around such questions for the many people who were present and then to publish the results of the conference for others who were not able to participate.[102]

The COVID-19 pandemic dominated the year 2020 around the world. Inevitably, the turmoil affected FATEB and the countries where its two campuses were located. Schools were closed in both Central African Republic and Cameroon. These closures included the seminary programs and the general education programs of the Bangui campus where over 3,000 children and youth had been attending school daily. The theological students in Bangui worked at home, though the excessive cost of an internet connection made it almost impossible to offer teaching online at that time.

Churches were closed, and any gathering of more than 15 people was forbidden in Bangui. Economically, church staffs suffered because their finances were based on the tithes and offerings collected during the Sunday services. This in turn impacted their support of students in training who lacked funds for their school fees and living expenses. Strict rules were established to protect the health of those living on campus. Guests were not allowed to come onto the grounds. Off campus, lock-down was almost impossible where people were living closely together. Hospitals were poorly

---

102. Jack Robinson, newsletter, 2.15.20.

equipped to respond to the pandemic, and some places lacked enough clean water to wash one's hands as recommended.[103]

With the schools closed to students, and the facilities and guest rooms unable to be rented out, local sources of income ran dry, making it difficult to pay FATEB salaries. Salaries of the leadership were cut from 70 percent to 50 percent, non-essential workers were laid off, and operational expenses were reduced except for water and electricity.[104]

With cases of the infection climbing, international agencies contributed thousands of protective masks to C.A.R. The government distributed them, insisting that they be worn in public places. The Women's School leaders made facial masks to help protect employees and students living on campus. The salaries of all existing FATEB employees were further reduced to 40 percent of pre-COVID salary levels.

Classes on the Cameroon campus resumed in June 2020, though social distancing was being practiced. On the Bangui campus, only students in their final year of the bachelor's program returned to campus to complete their degrees and graduate. To complete his graduation requirements, a doctoral student defended his dissertation before a jury via Zoom as his last hurdle before graduation.[105]

In late June 2020, churches received authorization to conduct services, but only if they observed the safety rules decreed by the government. President Touadéra came to FATEB's campus wearing a face mask and personally distributed 70,000 masks to the heads of 60 churches in Bangui. Dr. Nupanga wrote, "Although the seminary is officially closed, we are helping students in their final year to graduate in August 2020. We are expecting in Bangui 20 students who will get their bachelor's degree." In Cameroon, the master's students were able to graduate in August since the government had reopened its schools.[106]

As for the FATEB campus community, Dr. Nupanga wrote in September 2020, "Since March when the pandemic was detected in C.A.R., we took aggressive measures to avoid infection, but we believe God worked through these efforts to keep the campus community safe." He went on to write,

---

103. Jack Robinson, newsletter, 4.2.20.
104. Jack Robinson, newsletter, 4.28.20.
105. Jack Robinson, newsletter, 6.2.20.
106. Jack Robinson, newsletter, 6.25.20.

The government shut down FATEB's educational programs for almost four months. Yet, by the end of August, we were able to complete the academic year. The graduation ceremony took place on August 29th. More than a thousand people gathered for our celebration. The Minister of Higher Education joined the ceremony. We thank God that 28 men and women are ready to take up their ministries in five African countries: One graduated with a Ph.D. in New Testament, seven completed master's programs, fourteen received bachelor's degrees in theology, and six graduated from the Women's School. They will serve in Cameroon, Central African Republic, Chad, Democratic Republic of Congo, and Niger.[107]

FATEB had taken every precaution possible to prevent the spread of the COVID pandemic. Tests for the virus were readily available, and the few cases that appeared on campus resulted in immediate quarantine. The virus did not touch any of the hundreds of children in the campus schools, so the impact of the virus was minimal. Education of men, women, children, and youth continued throughout the dangerous months of the following year, 2021.

The schools for children and youth were reopened after a long closure. By the end of the 2019–2020 academic year, the students were able to complete their year's schoolwork and prepare to move on to their next grade in the following month. Their new school year began on October 15, 2020. With campus schools reopened, FATEB employees who had been laid off gradually returned to work. Seminary degree programs opened on October 12. In looking back over the previous months of crisis, Nupanga quoted the prophet Samuel, saying, "Thus far has the Lord helped us."

With the beginning of the new school year 2020–2021, Dr. Nupanga wondered how COVID-19 would affect new student enrollment. He was surprised with the outcome. In Bangui, forty-one students enrolled in the bachelor's program, seven in the master's track, and ten in the Women's School. In Yaoundé, 18 new students registered for bachelor's and master's studies, and 10 began doctoral work. Despite the COVID virus, 86 men and women came to classes in person.[108]

---

107. Jack Robinson, newsletter, 9.16.20.
108. Jack Robinson, newsletter, 12.2.20.

CHAPTER 6

Planning for the Future

2020–2021: ONLINE MASTER'S PROGRAM LAUNCHED

Throughout the final months of 2020, the COVID-19 pandemic compromised in-person learning everywhere. The need for student access to FATEB's educational programs from any location in central and west Africa was becoming more urgent. Adding online programs to the curriculum could make that possible, and for months prospective students in francophone Africa had been asking for them. In December 2020, FATEB leaders decided to begin online training. In February 2021, an online experimental course in pastoral theology commenced with 16 students. In March and April 2021, training of faculty members for online teaching began in preparation for first year courses in the master's program to be offered online later in the year. In this way, students anywhere in French-speaking Africa could enroll without leaving their places of residence.[1]

The first regular online master's classes were launched from the Cameroon campus in October 2021 under the direction of Dr. N'Kolo-Fanga. Dr. Nupanga hoped that soon there would be online students in all of Africa's French-speaking countries. The importance of the online project was underlined by the problems that the COVID pandemic had posed for in-person education.[2]

Further insecurity in C.A.R., including the danger for students in Bangui, made this new online initiative even more important. The country's president, Faustin Touadéra, had been reelected on December 27, 2020, to

---

1. Jack Robinson, newsletter, 2.2.20 and 3.2.21.
2. Jack Robinson, newsletter, 12.1.21.

Planning for the Future

a second five-year term. Enraged by the election results, rebels marched on the capital on January 13, 2021, attempting to overthrow the government. The National Army and its allies were able to push back the attack and prevent the rebels from entering the city. The rebels then put the capital under siege for the next ten weeks, cutting off the road from Cameroon to Bangui. In this land-locked country of C.A.R., the price of basic foods rose dramatically, and goods like flour, juices, and soap became unavailable. All the schools in Bangui were closed for ten days following the rebel attack, but the city itself remained protected. The seminary and other schools eventually reopened despite blockaded roads around the capital.[3]

The most demanding academic program at FATEB was at the doctoral level, and most of the doctoral students were directed from the Cameroon campus. The doctoral program could not have expanded as it did apart from several doctoral supervisors among the visiting professors who came from abroad. Eko Martin, a doctoral candidate who pastored a Presbyterian church and taught in a theological school in Cameroon, received his doctorate in May after being examined by a jury of specialists. His PhD dissertation focused on the role of elders in the local church and the way they provide congregational oversight. His purpose was to describe an ideal elder's role that would be faithful to biblical teaching but also would be properly attuned to African culture. What Martin learned through his research he hoped would result in greater harmony within the church and greater effectiveness in carrying out its mission in Africa.[4]

At the graduation ceremonies in 2021 on both campuses, 50 men and women celebrated the completion of their studies. Bachelor's, master's, and doctoral degrees were awarded, along with diplomas to graduates of the Women's School. Two government ministers attended the event in Bangui. The vice president of the Association of Evangelicals in Africa (AEA) addressed the graduates and their families and friends in Yaoundé. Hundreds of people attended the ceremonies on each campus. Dr. Nupanga reminded those present how important compassion was in the ministry of Jesus. His desire was that graduates be co-workers with Jesus as they lovingly guided people toward God.[5]

---

3. Jack Robinson, newsletter, 3.2.21.
4. Jack Robinson, newsletter, 6.17.21.
5. Jack Robinson, newsletter, 9.7.21.

2021–2022: STUDENT ENROLLMENT CONTINUES TO GROW

On October 11, 2021, student enrollment increased again. In C.A.R., 38 new students entered the bachelor's program (13 full time, 25 part time), 11 new students enrolled in the master's program, and 30 new students began classes on the Cameroon campus. More professional people were now studying part time in Bangui. A lawyer, a medical doctor, a high-ranking police officer, and other city leaders enrolled. In addition, 16 new students enrolled in the Women's School. Many of them were already well educated but chose the Women's School for the applied skills that women needed for family management and for employment opportunities.

On February 24, 2022, FATEB's corporate accountant, Floyd Bruning, passed away at the age of 93. Over the previous 20 years Bruning had worked on FATEB's accounts, first in Bangui and later in Yaoundé as well. Bruning assisted the seminary mainly from his home in Illinois (USA), though he made three trips to Bangui to help on-site with accounting and financial management. Bruning recommended that Marie-Angele Kosseke be appointed as FATEB's director of finance in 2021 and provided the initial orientation and training she needed for her complex responsibilities. Floyd Bruning's competent assistance and gentle spirit were an inspiration to all who worked with him. He is remembered with much gratitude.[6]

During FATEB's board of governors meeting in May 2022, a revised statement of the school's educational mission was adopted. Its aim is the "transformation of men, women and children for the building up of the Church and the well-being of society." The inclusion of the word "children" indicates that the general education schools that FATEB manages are to be considered an integral part of its overall mission, even though the primary focus remains on the seminary programs.

The online master's program that began in 2021 completed its first year. In April 2022, an Australian organization provided experts who led an in-service conference via Zoom for seminary faculty to better equip them for the challenge of teaching students both online and in person. All the faculty members and their assistants from the campuses in Yaoundé and Bangui participated in the training.[7]

---

6. Jack Robinson, newsletter, 3.25.22.
7. Jack Robinson, newsletter, 6.27.22.

PLANNING FOR THE FUTURE

On July 9, 2022, 48 men and women completed their studies at FATEB, to begin new paths of Christian service in Africa. Twenty-two finished the bachelor's program, thirteen earned their master's degrees, two were awarded the PhD, and eleven completed the Women's School program. The prime minister of C.A.R. was welcomed to campus during the graduation events. Despite political and military disruptions, 2022 marked the fortieth consecutive year of graduations since the first one was held in 1982.

2022–2024: FATEB'S 50-YEAR ANNIVERSARY OF ITS CHARTER

Following the graduation ceremony of 2022, FATEB organized a three-day conference on crisis leadership for one hundred leaders in the public and private sectors of the Central African Republic. Men, women, business leaders, pastors, and young leaders and FATEB students assembled on campus. The president of the country made a key presentation, sharing his experiences as head of state during the COVID-19 crisis. This conference offered a way of serving not only FATEB student leaders but also the wider society. Dr. Nupanga considered this conference a way of responding to Jesus' call to be the salt of the earth and the light of the world.[8]

At the end of 2022, Dr. Nupanga had served as doyen for 15 years. The Bangui campus had over 200 men and women in the degree programs at bachelor's, master's, and doctoral levels. Ten years had passed since the campus in neighboring Cameroon opened and where over one hundred students were enrolled at the same three academic levels as in Bangui. In the Women's School, 41 women were currently enrolled in the diploma programs designed for them. Online programs were in their second year with students from as far west as Senegal and from other countries in central Africa. Serving all of francophone Africa had been envisioned by FATEB's founders from the beginning, and online education was helping to make this possible, even in troubled political contexts.

The explosive growth of the Christian general education programs for children and youth was probably the biggest surprise for FATEB's leaders. In the 2022–2023 school year, 3,191 children and youth were enrolled. The quality of the education offered, and the Christian moral and spiritual values taught, brought public commendation from the country's president and expressions of appreciation from many parents.

8. Jack Robinson, newsletter, 9.13.22.

An African Dream

The nearly 50-year-old physical plant of FATEB was aging and badly needed maintenance and improvement. US-based Mtelo Ministries continued to invest thousands of hours, financial resources, and specialized skills in upgrading the campus facilities. Renovation of housing, upgrading electricity and plumbing, replacing flooring and window screens, installing a handicap ramp for disabled students and guests, outfitting a recording studio, paving the campus streets, and installing a proper trash burner for waste were among the many projects the Mtelo friends undertook. FATEB has always been a joint project of people from three continents working together to equip leaders for Christian ministry in French-speaking Africa.[9]

Because FATEB was founded to prepare students for applied ministries in churches and church-related institutions, the learning program was not designed to be only theoretical but practical as well. Thus, internships in the churches to provide students with opportunities for ministry experience constituted from the beginning an important dimension of the curriculum. In early 2023, the presidents of several Evangelical denominations in Bangui and about 100 pastors were invited to campus to evaluate the importance of internships for both students and churches. With 239 students enrolled in the university level programs of FATEB in 2023, the seminary needed many well managed internships in the city. At this conference, FATEB faculty and administrators explained to church leaders how they hoped the churches could provide positive learning experiences and spiritual support for the student interns they received. In turn, the church leaders gave constructive feedback to FATEB professors that helped them better prepare students for internship opportunities.[10]

Beginning with their second year in school, every student at FATEB in Bangui is assigned to an Evangelical church in the city to serve as an intern. Every spring semester, seminary staff and students visit about 150 churches to explain the work of FATEB and to encourage churches in their service to the local population. Many of these churches help to underwrite the costs of the seminary's educational programs.[11]

In February 2023, campus administrative leaders broke ground for the newest building project on the Bangui campus. This ceremony officially inaugurated the construction of a three-story high school (*lycée*) building of eighteen classrooms. The three-year FATEB *lycée* reached 1,100 students

---

9. Jack Robinson, newsletter, 12.15.22.
10. Jack Robinson, newsletter, 3.22.23.
11. Jack Robinson, newsletter, 6.27.23.

in 2022–2023 with the school classrooms currently scattered about the campus in three different buildings. The construction of a single building for high school students has already begun to assist both students and teachers to better coordinate their educational activities. Student fees from parents constituted the major financing for the new building. Providing Christian education for these young people has broadened the impact of FATEB's mission.[12]

To highlight biblical values for both students and other Christians in the city's churches, Dr. Nupanga organized a three-day conference on creation care in early May 2023. Living near the Great Congo Basin rainforest, people in the Central African Republic have watched the forests gradually disappearing. In the Bible, God is described as giving Adam responsibility to tend and watch over the garden of Eden. This conference, called "Garden of Eden Project," was designed to teach and show people how they could have a positive impact on the environments in which they live. FATEB is writing a curriculum for its general education schools that presents creation care as a way of thanking God for his lavish material blessings. Keeping the campus green and clean is one way the seminary community is modeling this value.[13]

Graduation ceremonies on both the Bangui and Cameroon campuses in July 2023 filled the students with joy. Together with their families, teachers, and the church leaders, they prayed for the future ministries that awaited them in French-speaking Africa. Fifty-three graduates from six different countries left FATEB to serve African churches and society: eighteen with bachelor's degrees, twenty with master's degrees, nine with diplomas from the Women's School, and six with PhDs.

In the fall of 2023, as the online master's program began its third year of classes, online students were enrolled from Madagascar in the east, Gabon in the south, Morocco in the north, and Côte d'Ivoire and Senegal in the west. The founders' dream of a school that would serve all of francophone Africa had become a reality.[14]

In February 2024, FATEB's 50-year anniversary was celebrated. In 1974, the C.A.R. government had authorized the establishment of FATEB in Bangui and granted it land for a seminary. For 50 years of God's faithfulness to the many members FATEB's community across the years, the

---

12. Jack Robinson, newsletter, 3.22.23.
13. Jack Robinson, newsletter, 3.22 and 6.27.23.
14. Jack Robinson, newsletter, 9.20.23.

assembly that gathered offered grateful thanks to God with the prayer that this institution would continue to strengthen Christ's church and its mission throughout francophone Africa for many years to come.[15]

---

15. Jack Robinson, newsletter, 9.20.23.

Afterword

THE STORY OF FATEB is not yet finished. The life of the seminary community continues. Perhaps someone in the future will pick up the narrative where this leaves off and continue to describe it. FATEB leaders have testified to the providence of God in preserving this institution through numerous challenges both internal and external. But they also realize that human actors will influence its direction in the months and years ahead, men and women in need of guidance to fulfill the seminary's mission.

In attempting to write an historical account of FATEB's past, I hope to provide information that would aid the leaders who will be directing it into the future. I hope that future leaders will understand the mission that brought FATEB into existence. Among the purposes for which FATEB was founded, there were three of special importance. First, FATEB was created to provide university level training for men and women who desired education that would equip them for a variety of Christian leadership responsibilities. This involved the maturing of their personal character, the deepening of their human relationships, and the acquisition of knowledge and skills they would need for future life and ministry. Second, FATEB was created to equip men and women for service in and to the churches and Christian institutions of francophone Africa. The Christian communities scattered throughout these African countries represent enormous potential for enabling their members to be growing, faithful disciples of Jesus Christ who could carry out their calling to be salt and light in African societies. Finally, FATEB was created to be an educational institution that would honor God by its commitment to love God and neighbor deeply as it carries out its mission.

Each generation will need to decide how best to fulfill FATEB's mission. This will mean that the seminary will continue to be reshaped to effectively serve churches and societies that are in a state of constant change.

Afterword

Most changes can be made without compromising the mission of FATEB. But some changes would indeed modify the seminary's primary purposes. There are voices that have already suggested that FATEB change its mission from preparing leaders specifically for churches and Christian organizations to preparing young people for more broad and diverse roles in society. This resembles the purpose of a Christian university, and it is a worthy purpose. But FATEB's mission has always been more focused. It was founded primarily to strengthen the churches and Christian institutions of French Africa. This is why people have invested in it for the past fifty years. Other voices have suggested that FATEB restrict itself to serving church and society mainly in the Central African Republic. This country needs national educational institutions with such a vision. But FATEB was founded to have a regional scope, to serve the churches in all of Africa's French-speaking countries, not just the country in which its campus was located.

In short, constant vigilance is required to keep an institution on the path for which it was created. The doyen, the board of governors, and the Association of Evangelicals in Africa have worked together to maintain the fidelity of FATEB to its original purpose and values through all the challenges it has faced over the past half century. I hope and pray that this brief historical sketch of FATEB's past will be helpful to its future leaders who will be charting its course. I hope it will also encourage its future friends and supporters to sustain their partnerships with this institution as it continues to form students for Christian life and service in the French-speaking countries of Africa.

APPENDIX

Western Christian Missionaries and African Christian Nationals at FATEB

IN 1873 THE SCOTTISH missionary and explorer David Livingstone died in Africa. What followed his death for the next 40 years was what became known as the "Scramble for Africa." Half a dozen European nations claimed vast areas of African territory, making them part of their colonial empires. By 1912 all of Africa was under European colonial rule except for Ethiopia and Liberia.

The European takeover of Africa led to Africans' loss of control over their own affairs and brought enormous hardship to most Africans. Many died because of the conquest itself and many others from the demographic disruptions that followed. Colonial rule brought about social, political, and economic change on the continent. Only slowly did African colonies gain their independence, most of them around 1960.

Many Christian missionaries from the West went to Africa following World War I. For the subsequent 40 years, these missionaries were perceived to be implicated in the colonial rule under which they also lived. But with political independence of African nations came a healthy transition from foreign missionary leadership of the churches to leadership by African Christians.

In 1973, one hundred years after the death of Livingstone, a new association comprising African evangelical national fellowships decided to establish two graduate schools of theology. One would serve the former French-speaking colonies and the other the former English-speaking colonies. Just as the new African nations had African political leaders, so the churches would have their own African spiritual and ecclesiastical leaders.

Appendix: Western Christian Missionaries

Furthermore, these church leaders would be trained mostly in Africa, by Africans, and for Africa. That is how FATEB, the francophone African training institution, was founded.

New African leadership resulted in radically changed patterns of foreign missionary roles on the continent. It was no longer a question of how Africans could serve the agenda of foreign missionaries. Rather, the critical question was how missionaries from abroad could contribute to ministries in Africa that reflected African approaches to Christian mission and do so under their leadership. Some foreign missionaries were able to make the adjustment, others were not. People in the missionary sending countries were often confused about what was really happening on the fields of missionary service.

In 1965, Theo and I began our service in Africa, functioning like pioneer missionaries before us had done for many decades. We did direct evangelism, discipleship, and church-planting ministries with minimal reference to the ideas and advice of African Christians. But in the new era of political independence, Africa was changing rapidly before our eyes. By 1971, we were working in collaboration with African Christian leaders, and in 1973 we began working under African leadership and have done so ever since.

Today, in 2025, relations between foreign missionaries and Christian nationals have changed from what they were in the past. We see this at FATEB where foreign personnel have very limited, part-time roles in educational and administrative functions. We have discovered that, as foreigners, we do not have to be, and generally should not be, the ones in charge of local programs and institutions. Our best contributions to the mission of the church in Africa are usually more supportive in character. It is deeply gratifying for us to see students whom we have taught at FATEB graduate and move into responsible roles as pastors, missionaries, teachers, translators, and leaders of denominations, of compassionate ministries, and of training institutions. We love these men and women and are proud of their commitments and accomplishments. We are grateful to be their friends and colleagues and to have an influence in their lives. But they are indeed the key to leading the African church in fulfilling its mission to the peoples of francophone Africa.

Appendix of Primary Sources

Adeyemo, Tokunboh, fax message to Jack Robinson, 1.10.95.
Africa's BEST, Inc. (ABI). Articles of incorporation, May 1984.
———. BEST annual board meeting report, 8.15.88.
———. BEST News of the Bangui Evangelical Graduate School of Theology, December 1983; October–December 1985; August–September 1987.
———. BEST news release, May 1985.
Alliance Evangélique en Centrafrique (AEC). Minutes of the AEC board meeting, 3.30.78.
Association of Evangelicals of Africa and Madagascar (AEAM). AEAM President Samuel Odunaike quote. *Afroscope* 13 (Oct. 1977) 4.
———. Minutes of the Executive Committee, 3.15–19.76; Nairobi, 8.2–4.79.
———. Minutes of the Second General Assembly. Limuru, Kenya, 1973.
———. Minutes of the Theological Commission and Action Committee, Bangui, 7.7–10.75.
———. Minutes of the Third General Assembly, Bouaké, Côte d'Ivoire, 7.30–8.2.77.
———. Press Release: "Africa Evangelicals Offered Choice Property by President of the Central African Republic." 3.20.74.
———. Report of FATEB cornerstone laying ceremony. *Afroscope* (Aug. 1975) 1.
———. Theological Conference, Theological Commission and minutes, 11.21–26.75.
Baker, Milton, letter to Byang Kato, 10.6.75.
———. Letter to Jack Robinson and the heads of EFMA and IFMA, 10.6.75.
Bass, John, fax message to Jack Robinson, 5.22.96.
Bennett, John, West Africa trip report, 4.29–5.7.94.
Best, Anna, letter to Isaac Zokoué, 4.15.88.
———. Letter to Jack Robinson, 2.20.91.
———. Newsletters, July 1989; November 1989; 1.16.1990.
Bruning, Floyd, letter to Jack Robinson, 10.1.01.
———. Letter to Abel Ndjérarèou, 12.3.01.
Central African Republic Government. "Ordonnance No 74/025, autorisant la création d'une Faculté privée de Théologie [Ordinance No. 74/025, Authorizing the Creation of a Private Theological School]." 2.27.74.
Daidanso, René, Isaac Zokoué, Don Hocking, letter to Jack Robinson, Paul White, Tite Tiénou, Byang Kato, 8.31.74.
Dangers, Jack, letters to Jack Robinson, 9.23.74; October 1974.
Dillon, Robert, letter to Byang Kato, 10.22.74.
Doko-Manga, letter to the president of the AEAM executive committee, 3.30.78.

Appendix of Primary Sources

FATEB. Brochure, 1982.
———. Minutes of the board of governors meeting, Bangui, 12.29.78–1.1.79.
———. Press Release: "A New President at Bangui Evangelical Graduate School of Theology." September 2000.
Fleming, Bruce, letter to Allen Lutz, 10.18.84.
———. Letter to friends, 8.28.85.
———. Letter to Jack Robinson, 10.7.86.
———. Newsletters, September–October 1985; October–December 1985; October 1986.
Grace Brethren. "President of the Central African Republic Donates Property to Africa's Evangelicals." Press release, Bangui, March 1974.
Graves, Jack, Overseas Council letter to ABI related people, 1.10.89.
Hill, Judy, newsletter, 1992.
Hocking, Don, letters to Jack Robinson, 6.10.73; 11.26.73; 8.12.74; 4.14.75; 8.31.75.
———. Letter to Byang Kato, 1.7.74.
———. Letter to John Zielasko, Grace Brethren Mission, 10.14.75.
Howard, David M. Report to the AEAM General Council, 6.17–18.83.
———. World Evangelical Fellowship statement on BEST, 5.10.84.
Kato, Byang H. "The BEST for Africa." Spring 1975.
———. Letter to Don Hocking, 10.24.74.
———. Rough estimates of initial costs at Bangui, 12.31.74.
Kennedy, Alistair, letters to Jack Robinson, 10.26.73; 2.6.74.
Kohl, Manfred, report on FATEB, May 1995.
Koudougueret, David, faculty report, April 2001.
Landrud, Ken, letter to Jack Robinson, 3.9.96.
Lea, Herb, newsletters, April 1985; 6.8.85; 8.28.85.
Lea, Susan, report, 1986.
Maillefer, Eric. Mini-rapport sur l'Assemblée Générale AEAM [mini-report on the AEAM General Assembly], undated.
Marini-Bodho, Dirindo, letter to Paul White, 10.8.79.
Mokoko, Adé, BEST children's school report, 1987.
Naramore, Kathy, letter to Jack Robinson, 3.1.89.
Odunaike, Samuel, letter to Doko-Manga, president of AEC, 4.8.78.
———. Letter to Isaac Zokoué, president of the FATEB board of governors, 4.8.78.
———. Letter to Paul White, doyen of FATEB, 4.8.78.
Paluku, Josaphat. FATEB Information Bulletin no. 14, December 1984.
———. Letter to FATEB friends, 12.30.83.
———. Letter to Van Barneveld, 3.21.84.
———. Newsletter no. 11, March 1983.
Penney, Don, letter to René Daidanso, 1.7.91.
Robinson, Jack. ABI President's Report, June 1987.
———. Biographical sketch of Dr. Nupanga Weanzana, 2007.
———. Email to Isaac Zokoué, 1.31.97.
———. Future ministry proposal, 7.31.93.
———. "Interview with Dr. Jack Robinson, President of the Conservative Baptist Seminary of the East, Regarding Theological Education in French-Speaking Africa," 9.22.88.
———. Letter to Byang Kato, 8.5.74.
———. Letters to friends, 4.1.84; March 1989; 1.2.97.

Appendix of Primary Sources

———. Letter to Jim Plueddemann, 7.31.93.
———. Letter to John Bennett, 6.10.94.
———. Letters to Manfred Kohl, 3.12.94; late 2001.
———. Letter to René Daidanso, 1.12.95.
———. Newsletters, Fall 1993; January 1996; July 1996; October 1996; 1.2.97; 6.13.97; 8.8.97; 10.21.97; 4.15.98; 7.15.98; November 1998; January 1999; April 1999; June 1999; February 2000; January 2001; October 2001; January 2002; April 2002; June 2002; November 2002; January 2003; March 2003; May 2003; August 2003; 2.18.04; 5.12.04; 7.26.04; 8.18.04; 10.9.04; 2.24.05; 7.14.05; 2.20.06; 5.3.06; 9.18.06; 1.2.07; 10.26.07; 4.17.07; 7.7.07; 9.26.07; 12.4.07; 2.7.08; 3.4.08; 5.2.08; 7.30.08; 12.9.08; 7.10.09; 9.29.09; 5.6.10; 6.19.10; 9.8.10; 12.4.10; May 2011; 7.29.11; 10.26.11; 2.23.12; 7.20.12; 10.4.12; 11.28.12; 2.5.13; 3.30.13; 5.1.13; 6 25.13; 8.8.13; 10.29.13; 12.24.13; 2.8.14; 4.17.14; 9.25.14; 2.16.15; 11.11.14; 1.16.15; 3.31.15; 7.8.15; 12.1.15; 2.5.16; 8.19.16; 11.16.16; 2.3.17; 9.11.17; March 2018; May 2018; 8.27.18; 12.11.18; 3.8.19; 5.22.19; 8.12.19; 11.20.19; 2.15.20; 4.2.20; 4.28.20; 6.2.20; 6.25.20; 9.16.20; 12.2.20; 2.2.20; 3.2.21; 6.17.21; 9.7.21; 3.25.22; 6.27.22; 9.13.22; 12.15.22; 3.22.23; 6.27.23; 9.20.23.
———. Notes on construction plans, 1.27.98.
———. Notes on conversations with Isaac Zokoué, 6.6.94; 9.6.94; 12.6.94.
———. Project proposal for FATEB, 11.1.93.
———. Report on the National Reconciliation in Central African Republic, email, 3.16.98.
———. Reports on FATEB/BEST, September 1984; 4.1.89.
———. Trip Report, 2000.
Schmidt, Paul, letter to Jack Robinson, 12.12.95.
Shank, Floyd, letter to Paul White, 6.16.78.
———. Cover letter to the FATEB board of governors and president of AEAM, 6.23.78.
Students of FATEB, letter to Dirindo Marini-Bodho, 8.2.78.
———. Letter to FATEB board of governors, 3.25.78.
———. *Phos* 4 (June 1984); *Phos* 6 (1986); *Phos* not numbered (June 1985).
United States Embassy in Central African Republic. Excerpt from a Central African Republic Country Report on Human Rights Practices for 1997. Published by the Bureau of Democracy, Labor and Human Rights, 1.30.98.
———. Possible Embassy recommendations for U.S. Citizens, 4.26.96.
University of Strasbourg, letter to Isaac Zokoué, 6.9.94.
Walkup, John. ABI, Friends in Touch, 1986; October 1987.
———. Letter to Jack Robinson, 4.18.88.
———. Memo to the ABI board, 1.4.89.
Weanzana, Nupanga, letter to Isaac Zokoué, 4.4.95.
———. Letter to Jack Robinson, 12.11.95.
———. Newsletters to FATEB friends, 6.15.97; January 2008.
White, Arline, letter to friends, 6.1.79.
———. Report on the formation of all the family at FATEB, January 1980.
White, Paul. B.E.S.T. Information, 11.1.77.
———. Communiqué to the FATEB board of governors, 12.2.77.
———. FATEB Information Bulletin no. 3, July 1978; no. 4, December 1978; no. 5, May 1979; no. 6, January 1980; not numbered, July 1980; no. 14, December 1984.
———. Letter to Byang Kato and the Theological Commission, 3.8.75.

Appendix of Primary Sources

———. Letters to friends, 11.1.77; 9.9.78; January 1981; 10.4.81; 3.30.82; 11.7.82; 3.26.83; 7.5.83.
———. Letters to Jack Robinson, 7.22.75; 9.17.75.
———. Letters to members of the AEA Theological Commission, 4.25.75; 6.5.75.
———. Letters to members of the FATEB General Assembly, 7.20.76; 7.31.78; 8.23.78.
———. Letter to missions with work in Francophone Africa, 1.23.76.
———. Letters to students, 1.27.77; 7.1.77; 7.8.77.
———. Letter to John Zielasko, 4.19.78.
———. Newsletter, 10.20.75; November 1976; 12.6.77; 6.15.78.
Zielasko, John, letter to Paul White, 4.19.78.
Zokoué, Isaac. FATEB President's Reports, November 1999; December 2000; April 2001.
———. Fax messages to Jack Robinson, 12.23.96; 1.25.97.
———. Five-year plan, March 1987.
———. "The Founding of FATEB." Unpublished interview by Jack Robinson, 11.28.06.
———. Letter to FATEB General Assembly, 3.28.78.
———. Letter to Harold Alexander, director of overseas ministries, Worldteam, 7.29.78.
———. Letter to Jack Robinson, 12.2.93.
———. Letter to Paul White, February 1975.
———. Newsletter, December 1993.
———. Proposal for resolving conflicts within FATEB, 8.31.78.
———. Report on the 1993–1994 year.
———. Strategic Planning—July 2000; April 2001.
———. Summary of the state of FATEB, 1992.

Bibliography

Associated Press. "World News Briefs: French Troops Support Central African Republic." *New York Times*, April 20, 1996.
Breman, Christina Maria. *The Association of Evangelicals in Africa: Its History, Organization, Members, Projects, External Relations and Message.* Zoetermeer: Utigeverij Boekencentrum, 1996.
Calver, Clive. *The Evangelicals.* Milton Keynes, UK: Paternoster, 1986.
Frizen, Edwin L., Jr. *Seventy-Five Years of IFMA, 1917-1992: The Nondenominational Missions Movement.* Pasadena: William Carey Library, 1992.
Howard, David M. *The Dream That Would Not Die: The Birth and Growth of the World Evangelical Fellowship 1946-1986.* Milton Keynes, UK: Paternoster, 1986.
Kato, Byang H. *Byang H. Kato 1936-1975: Perspectives of an African Theologian: The Writings of Byang H. Kato Th.D.* ACTEA, compact disc, n.d.
———. *Theological Pitfalls in Africa.* Kisumu, Kenya: Evangel, 1975.
———. *Pièges Théologiques en Afrique.* Translated by N. de Mestral-Demole. Abidjan: Centre de Publications Evangéliques, 1981.
———. "Theological Trends in Africa Today." *Perception* 1.1 (Mar. 1974) 1-9.
Maillefer, Eric. *Memoirs of Eric Maillefer: To Forget Is to Not Belong.* Unpublished manuscript. Huntley, IL: 2009.
Nossiter, Adam. "Violent and Chaotic, Central African Republic Lurches Toward a Crisis." *New York Times*, Aug. 6, 2013, 1.
Wikipedia. "2003 Central Africa Republic Coup d'Etat." https://en.wikipedia.org/wiki/2003_Central_African_Republic_coup_d%27%C3%A9tat.
———. "François Bozizé." https://en.wikipedia.org/wiki/Fran%C3%A7ois_Boziz%C3%A9.

www.ingramcontent.com/pod-product-compliance
Lightning Source LLC
Chambersburg PA
CBHW072138160426
43197CB00012B/2155